LEARNING CHAOS

HOW DISORDER CAN SAVE EDUCATION

How to Contact the Author

Mac Bogert spreads Learning Chaos—every chance he gets—through assessments, leadership coaching, and learning opportunities for associations, schools, teachers groups and other organizations worldwide. Contact Mac with queries and comments at macbogert@azalearning.com. Listen to Mac's conversations with learners—from school kids to award-winning authors—at the Learning Chaos Podcast.

Acclaim for Author and Educator, Mac Bogert

"I have watched Mac Bogert numerous times as he led classes in a variety of leadership topics. Mac takes learning seriously enough to enjoy every moment. Participants leave his sessions alight with a new curiosity and respect for challenging ideas. Learning Chaos captures this enthusiasm and brings his insight to the critical dilemma of our schools. Bravo!"

—Kirke Harper, Director (retired) of the Leadership
Development Academy at the Graduate School, USDA

"Mac Bogert's work is important for our time, since changing the classroom means changing our habits of thinking. Learning Chaos is not only timely and relevant, it's fun to read."

—Sir John Hargrave, author of *Mind Hacking: How to Change
Your Mind for Good in 21 Days*

"Mac plays blues guitar, sails, and ... Hell, there is little he can't do. His passion is infectious. But Mac always comes back to what shapes him. He's a teacher. More important, he is a learner. Learning Chaos is a good read and an important book that will forever change how we view education."

—Robert Ward, author, screenwriter, producer

I met Mac when we worked together during a major organizational change at the U.S. Department of Education. I'm not surprised that Learning Chaos is full of surprises. The book is a reflection of his willingness to challenge any practice that impedes learning.

—Gail Hanson, Vice President of Campus Life,
American University

I have always been passionate about leadership and sustainability. The goal of Learning Chaos parallels my own—sustainable, lifelong learning. The book balances humor and careful research toward a revolution in education.

—Greg Balestrero, Strategic Advisor for the International
Institute for Learning; author, *Organizational Survival:
Profitable Strategies for a Sustainable Future*

LEARNING CHAOS

HOW DISORDER CAN SAVE EDUCATION

MAC BOGERT

AZA Learning

Annapolis, Maryland

Book design by Frances Keiser, Sagaponack Books & Design

ISBN: 978-0-9963018-0-0 (softcover)
ISBN: 978-0-9963018-1-7 (e-book)
Library of Congress Catalog Card Number: 2015908013

Summary: Learning Chaos is a new approach to education that identifies the barriers that inhibit learning in today's schools and demonstrates how to overturn them through Discovery, Assembly, Skepticism and Fluidity. The book also provides suggestions for improving classroom management and redefines a teacher's role in harnessing curiosity—the default setting for all students.

EDU034000 Education / Educational Policy & Reform / General
EDU012000 Education / Experimental Methods
EDU036000 Education / Organizations & Institutions

AzaLearning.com

Aza Learning
Annapolis, Maryland

Printed and bound in USA
First Edition

For MacBeth, the name we used to help people remember the two of us together and to get a laugh. This book, like our lives, was everything of both of us. What's gone cannot come back, but what's here will always be. Thanks, Beth for our life.

my teachers,
the legion of intersections
that confused shocked bored enlightened
both ways I'd guess
intent or accident
They
threw chaos
to plant the seeds
weeds or garden,
the same thing

"I never let my schooling interfere with my education."

—Mark Twain

ACKNOWLEDGEMENTS

Nine years ago I woke up with Learning Chaos in my head. The idea and the title appeared at the same time like mysterious lodgers. You're looking at the result of a long line of iterations and revisions, all of which came back to the same idea: we underestimate the capacity of children and adults—tall children—for learning. Nothing in my decades of teaching, whether with kids, teenagers, or adults, contradicts the notion that people want to learn and have a huge reservoir of untapped discovery. They simply need permission.

School and I had a love-hate relationship. I held nothing back in classes led by teachers who challenged me. The other 75% taught me how to doze in class without getting caught and wrote "does not work up to his potential" on my report card. As a student, I wore out the linoleum cooling my heels outside the principal's office. As a teacher, too.

In college I jettisoned the mediocrity of my first two years when a literature professor challenged me to stop goofing off and learn. I realized then that not every teacher can be great, and that I wouldn't expect greatness from every teacher—I would look for great learning regardless. I continue to seek great learning. And chaos encourages learning. Not everyone—most teachers and administrators—have seen that truth with the same clarity I do.

With the Internet, there's no excuse for mediocre learning. The time is ripe for a complete overhaul of the traditional concept of schooling. Our learning switch is always on. Learning Chaos focuses on removing the barriers that short-circuit our default setting: to learn.

I owe the evolution of this book to many people.

Since every interaction sparks learning, I'd like to thank everyone I've ever known. Because space dictates brevity, I've shortened the list.

Gratitude to:

Beth Rubin, my editor, chief balloon-popper ("What the hell is this chapter supposed to be about?") and source of ongoing support.

Beth Mansbridge, the Queen of Copy Editing and dispenser of subtle feedback ("I'm not sure that *horse shit* is appropriate for your intended audience").

Frances Keiser, who led me through the mysteries of formatting and pre-publication; ever patient, untiring, and focused.

Ralph Lobosco, who during a phone conference in 2010, said (with others listening in), "Whatever happened to that book you said you were writing?" Ouch, and thanks for the nudge. I needed it.

Greg Balestrero, Ken Karsten, Lew Taylor, Fred Bogert, Carol Smith, Robert Ward, Lex Birney, and Gail Hansen all helped me to move forward.

Angel, who stood sentry and forced me to get out of the chair for occasional walks.

DINOSAURS IN PRISONS

Drive by a medium-security prison. Take away the razor wire, add a mascot, and what do you have? A public school. They both contain people whose attendance is mandatory. Both are managed by a top-down hierarchy. When challenged by change, both generate more rules. There are some differences: You can't be expelled from prison. Prisoners can't pack a lunch. Children can't appeal their sentence.

Schools and prisons look alike because they are alike. Nature, engineering, and architecture all follow the maxim that form follows function. So a bird's wing and a plane's wing have a lot in common. Purpose generates design. We pick up a sharp piece of flint and notice that it looks like a knife. Their shared purpose generates their congruent design. Dogs' noses have flaps that channel their exhalation sideways. That way they don't disturb what they're sniffing. We don't have those flaps (most of us, anyhow) because we don't need those flaps. The basic shape of schools hasn't evolved much because the basic principles of education haven't. Their primary purpose has been, and still is, to control and correct.

House of correction is a euphemism for prisons. A medieval *gaol* (jail) on a hilltop in Turkey follows the same functional necessity as a county detention center in Maryland. Like turtles and tortoises, they are more alike than different. And that necessity limits the evolution of schools. The more schools focus on regulating learners, the more they resemble *houses of correction*. The evolution is clear: the newer the school, the fewer the windows, the wider the moat (parking lots), and the more ubiquitous the closed-circuit monitors. Security concerns, uniform standards, and diminished respect for teachers support a mechanistic approach to building schools and, more important, to what happens in them. So schools, bus schedules, and curricula are organized for efficiency, like factories. Or prisons. In 1940 there were 117,000 school districts in the United States. By 1990, that number had shrunk to 15,000[1]. More efficient? Perhaps. Cost effective? Arguable. More creative? Hardly.

This theme of control and uniformity influences what's taught as well. Test scores are principal in every public school as well as in most private schools. Test scores determine political support, real estate desirability, and *funding*. Test scores confine learning like a straitjacket, as though we graduate to a world of standardized tests and rote memorization. The focus on tests is merely a symptom of a greater blindness.

Schools can't succeed in producing the kind of learners we need, and will need more every year, if we merely tinker—impose merit pay, adjust teacher certification, add in-service days, strengthen / throw out tenure, create new administrative units, reduce class size, increase class size, remove classroom walls, put the walls back, promote creativity, institute *back to basics*, withdraw funding from low performers, pay students for achieving, eliminate recess, or pad student GPAs for skipping bathroom breaks. Does the last sound a bit farfetched? In 2006, this practice was recommended to improve achievement in several high schools in Fairfax County, Virginia, one of the top-rated school districts in the nation.

We are in the habit of throwing solutions against a wall and hoping one sticks. What we're throwing may or may not have value. The quality of the solution is immaterial because we're throwing it against the wrong walls. No new idea can find much life inside a detention center. So we look for someone to blame: It's the teachers! It's the parents! It's the federal government! It's the '60s! It's the children!

There are no villains here, just dinosaurs—ideas fossilizing everywhere in the real world, yet still flourishing in schools. These dinosaur ideas include the immense *top-down*-osaurus, the lumbering *test*ocodopus, and the mindless *control*odactyl, among others. They belong in museums as objects of curiosity, not roaming school hallways squashing it. These ideas were behind the times fifty years ago. The growing pains that pummeled public schools in the second half of the 20th century—integration, self-esteem, student-teacher ratios, the rise of the National Education Association (NEA), the explosion of post-secondary cost—all reflected waves caused by a seismic change in thinking and learning—until the next wave came along. All these waves, good or otherwise, broke against the retaining walls of our educational assumptions and left the walls largely intact.

The rise of open-source technology such as Wikipedia and Linux, the democratization of information through the Web, and the spectacular speed of idea flow and change may scare some. These changes may signal the end of a simpler time. But these changes are here, and new ones are arriving at increasing velocity, too fast for tuning. Adjustments won't fix a system that has changed little since dismissal times were coordinated with crop harvests.

"Build it and they will come" is about rebuilding to attract a new *they*. And *they* are new ideas, generated in a new, holistic environment that enables learning flow by deconstructing barriers. What are these barriers? *Any* part of schooling that impedes the flow of ideas. Flow introduces transparency and useful chaos, like tides in the ocean that are necessary to life—in this case, the life of thinking.

The fractured flow of ideas in public schools impedes the life of thinking. These impediments include classrooms; grades; grade levels; a uniform curriculum; departments; districts; time periods; and separation of teachers, students, and administrators. They go against every bit of current research on brain function, cognition, and emotional intelligence. Learning is organic, inclusive, boundless, and harmonic, "not like the parts in a machine but like the instruments in a symphony orchestra combining their tenor, volume, and resonance to create a particular musical effect."[2] That musical effect needs rehearsal space— classrooms—designed for *symphony (sounding together)*.

Once that symphony becomes the desired state, schools can be reverse-engineered with a new generation in mind, not only a new generation of learners, a new generation of ideas. These ideas need not be threatening. It's not about belief. Wherever you stand on Darwinism versus creationism, it's clear that things change. We change. The weather changes. Change moves away from one set of parameters and toward another. But the dinosaur ideas—memorization, right or wrong answers, competition—that generate the philosophy of incarceration have been locked in place for decades and longer. Attendance is mandatory. If schools are such great places, why do we punish misbehavior by making students stay longer? Detention is the ultimate terror. How many otherwise intelligent parents have bought into the crazy idea that taking their children out of school is not merely bad, but that it meddles with their kids' futures? Even if it's for an adventure such as travel (a.k.a. extracurricular learning).

Do schools reward learning? Not really. They reward accumulation and regurgitation. That's not the same as capacity. Grades, promotion, attendance, tests (including the SAT and the rest of the regurgitate-for-profit bunch), and awards all measure what students have *gathered*, not their capacity to gather in the future. That leads to forcing our youngest learners, those with "lantern consciousness,"[3] to turn off their capacity early and focus on pre-admission exercises (to an Ivy League school) that cauterize their curiosity.

This philosophy, focused on testing, misses the point that capacity can't be taught. It can only be learned. When we force inquisitive minds into the acquisition of rote learning, we do indeed ready them for school. They arrive on the first day of school pre-programmed for incarceration. That's right. Barely out of diapers, they have already accumulated a list of check-offs for admittance to pre-pre-pre-school. No time off for good behavior. Perhaps a long time ago, that kind of rote repetition made sense. It doesn't work now.

Before written language we carried information around with us internally. Writing (and reading) allowed us to archive information, to safeguard numbers and messages, and opened possibilities for commerce, history, and tradition. Writing and reading also created the opportunity for a new, exclusive class. Learning these skills was not easy; few could master them. So schools arose. Some focused on *democratizing* reading: The humanist impulse. Others focused on *controlling* reading: The exclusive impulse.[4] The education movement has always had these twin threads—democracy and control. The point of Learning Chaos is to derail the second. By focusing on capacity and information engineering, we can reduce control and flatten access. After all, in a cloud-based data universe there is no practical limit to information and knowledge access.

> What's unsurprising today would have seemed preposterous just fifteen years ago: an English-speaking thirteen-year-old in Zaire who's connected to the Internet can find the current temperature in Brussels or the closing price of IBM stock or the name of Winston Churchill's second finance minister as quickly and easily as the head librarian at Cambridge University.[5]

We're experiencing such a quantum growth in access that the profit-through-control motive may be the greatest dinosaur of all. It's not information that schools and teachers need to provide, it's information engineering, the technical term for *meaning*. We're not starved for information, we're starved for stories, the stickiest of learning experiences. And stories can be passed on without teaching. Simply sharing a story invites learning.

Teaching and learning have always coexisted, though not always functionally. We can learn because of teaching; we can also learn in spite of teaching, because teaching and learning are fundamentally different. The chart on the next page suggests a continuum along a line between pure teaching and pure learning. The two are symbiotic. The chart is about balance. The left side is more disciplined and academic, the right side more chaotic and fluid.

Learning is better than teaching because it is more intense; the more is being taught, the less can be learned.[6]

Taught	**Learned**
Navigation	Seamanship
Acting	Improv
Statistical Analysis	Meaning
Management	Leadership
Right Answers	Possibilities
Rigor	Interest
Jokes	Humor
Thoughtfulness	Mindfulness
Planning	Preparation
Reasonableness	Sanity
Storytelling	Stories

When the left-hand column dominates, it generates a fear of ambiguity, the illusion of control, a suspicion that fun has no place in learning, and the notion that laughter shows disrespect rather than surprise. It implies that authority is the antidote to the risk of uncontrolled curiosity. It's the penitentiary mindset—prisons and dinosaurs intersecting. Learning Chaos is about keeping the right-hand column as the goal in every school, finding every opportunity, no matter how unconventional, to give way to learning. First and always, to give way to the beauty of unexpected connections, "wild geysers of creative energy."

> The psychologist Dean Simonton argues that [this] fecundity ("wild geysers of creative energy") is often at the heart of what distinguishes the truly gifted. The difference between Bach and his forgotten peers isn't necessarily that he had a better ratio of hits to misses. The difference is that the mediocre might have a

dozen ideas, while Bach, in his lifetime, created more than a thousand full-fledged musical compositions. A genius is a genius, Simonton maintains, because he can put together such a staggering number of insights, ideas, theories, random observations, and unexpected connections that he almost inevitably ends up with something great. "Quality," Simonton writes, "is a probabilistic function of quantity."[7]

Schools need to become hotbeds of exploration and ideas. They may not manufacture Bachs and Einsteins, but they must provoke creative ideas in large enough numbers to engender a "probabilistic function of quantity" rather than a critical mass of regurgitation. In this environment, questions are more important than answers, ambiguity replaces certainty, and there are no wrong answers, only increasing possibilities.

Curriculum must *dis*organize and evolve through currents of diverse ideas. In the spirit of democracy, these currents must apply to administrators, teachers, staff, and students—universally and without bias. After all, capacity exists outside of accumulation. A degree from a university represents significant accomplishment; it may not signal significant *capacity*. Everybody in the building has one job. To learn.

Chaos is necessary to short-circuit the delusion of control that still dominates learning in schools. In fact, that delusion dominates most of our organizations. That delusion promotes fear, and that fear stifles the tendencies that make us human—primarily, the basic need for unfettered exploration. Learning Chaos confronts that fear, embracing the paradoxical safety of uncertainty. The more schools are planned and ordered, the less students can explore.

Exploration is the default setting for the human brain. Over millions of years, we have been on the alert, learning and investigating. We're infernally curious, asking "What if …?" when we see even the possibility of possibility. To scratch this itch, we invent and create. We are the only creatures that continually and consciously shape our environment, for good or ill. Balancing this exploratory need has always been the need for security in a world well stocked with things stronger and much faster than we are. For millennia, fueled by instinct and adrenaline, we fought through emergencies by running for cover, grabbing a stick in deathly desperation, the stick become a club, an ax, a spear, an atlatl[8], a bow, a rifle, a cannon, the atomic bomb. We invented to protect ourselves, to survive.

Today, this pressured kind of exploration—stress, anxiety, fear, competition, survival, eat or be eaten—is misappropriated in schools and in the workplace with grades, tests, measured achievement, college applications, job interviews, firing, and performance appraisals. It replicates the panther world where a moment's inattention, even in reflection, might impede the adrenaline stream. The fact is, we don't need to climb trees anymore; panthers are rare and elusive. So why do we impose pressure on ourselves, and worse, on our children, to perform? Why does learning only count if it meets an imposed standard? If curiosity's our default setting, we don't need to *make* learning happen. Yet schools persist in developing impediments to *intrinsic* learning. As educators, we need to get out of the way and let the innate hunger for learning prevail. It will always happen because it's the human condition. Schools, in trying to impose learning, impede learning.

The reason for learning anything, whether it's guitar, Guitar Hero, or Mandarin Chinese, isn't perfection or virtuoso skill. The motive is far simpler: bliss. Learning makes us happy and it provides us with feelings of control and novelty that are crucial to our psyches. "Maybe, just maybe," Gary Marcus says, "the art of reinvention and acquiring new skills can give us a sense of a life well lived."[9]

Schools are still replicating the law of the veldt where we dared not lose, so we dared not risk bona fide exploration—discovery motivated by curiosity and reflection, not by fear. We're still afraid of deviation from these fear-based rules, as if those rules still reliably protect us from claws and teeth. In that survival-ordered world, anything new *might* be a threat, so it's best avoided. That mindset is still so prevalent that it litters our language:

Better safe than sorry. ... Mind your business. ... A stitch in time saves nine. ... Better the evil you know. ... Perfect planning prevents piss-poor performance. ... Have a safe trip. ... Be careful out there. ... Let's not reinvent the wheel here. ... If it's not broken, don't fix it. ... Do it to them before they do it to you. ... Winning isn't the best thing, it's the only thing. ... F is for failure. ... Caution, curves in road. ....

We feed this withdrawal from our own best nature of fearless imagination every day with habits and words left over from the panther world, the world of protection in trees, caves, the *boma*[10], fortified villages, castles, moats ... and schools.

Learning Chaos is about introducing a safe level of disorder. Why? Because the world has changed; panthers no longer roam. Fear is no longer a useful catalyst. In a setting based on the principles of Learning Chaos, the motor of exploration develops internally; it's not imposed and restricted by authority. In a community of shared learning, we can explore and develop our native ability to question, seek, and construct. That natural, innate learning rests on the first of the four principles of Learning Chaos: discovery.

—◦◦◦◦—

1. This statistic and all others, unless noted otherwise, come from the National Center for Education Statistics, whose website, nces.ed.gov, provides a rich source of information and reference.

2. James Shreve, author of *The Genome War* and *The Neanderthal Enigma*, taken from "Beyond the Brain" in the *National Geographic*, March 2005.

3. From Alison Gopnik (*The Philosophical Baby: What Children's Minds Tell Us about Truth, Love, and the Meaning of Life*), quoted by David Brooks in *The Social Animal* (Random House, 2011). Lantern consciousness, Brooks writes "… illuminated outward in all directions—a vivid panoramic awareness of everything." Adults have "searchlight consciousness," focused on specifics. Brooks notes lantern behavior in the child in his story: "Harold wasn't observing, he was immersing." (pp. 45–46).

4. Jared Diamond cites compelling evidence in *Guns, Germs, and Steel* (W. W. Norton and Co., 1999), that early writing had very few symbols because it was only for limited use by the select. He quotes Claude Lévi-Strauss, the anthropologist, as saying early writing was intended "to facilitate the enslavement of other human beings." (p. 235). That impulse goes against most of our modern assumptions about language, but may still hold water when it comes to the purpose of education, at least in its inception.

5. Daniel H. Pink, in *A Whole New Mind* (Riverhead Books, 2006), pp. 102–103.

6. Josef Albers (1888–1976), born in Germany, taught at the Bauhaus until it was closed by the newly ascendant Nazi Party. He was a designer, photographer, printmaker, and poet, and he revolutionized art instruction after coming to the United States in 1933.

7. Malcolm Gladwell, from "Creation Myth," *The New Yorker*, May 16, 2011.

8. The atlatl is a grooved stick held in the thrower's hand, which gives a spear greater range and penetrating power.

9. Nick Owchar, in his review of *Guitar Zero* by Gary Marcus, in the *Los Angeles Times*, reprinted in the *Miami Herald*, Feb. 19, 2012.

10. *Boma* is a Bantu term for a circle of thorn bushes, usually erected as a temporary shelter to protect cattle and people from predators, especially lions. Oddly, it also seems to relate to a Persian word, leading to some interesting speculation about African history.

1: DISCOVERY

Just as the poets and writers described, we're going to be able to see, I think, that wondrous openness, utter and complete openness, of the mind of a child. In investigating the child's brain, we're going to uncover deep truths about what it means to be human, and in the process, we may be able to help keep our own minds open to learning for our entire lives.[1]

Discovery drives our first breath: *Wah!* Talk about a fall from grace. We're shocked by a sudden flood of information. We *notice*, the first step to every discovery for the rest of our lives.

Our skin develops touch. Fingers and toes wiggle as they prepare to grasp and to run. Eyes track movement and try to decipher distant shapes. Taste and smell find milk, the scents of mother and father. The waterfall of noise takes on association and direction, with a budding frustration for all that's beyond our reach. We want to discover more. Here isn't enough. We want to get *there*.

Finally, we explorers attain our greatest gift—locomotion. The pursuit begins. To protect the out-of-control explorer, Mom and Dad's guardian instincts mushroom. With the toddler's best interest—safety—at heart, they start childproofing. They erect barriers to prevent little Columbus from falling off the edge of the world. The battle escalates: a seesaw between the child's need for discovery and the parents' need for control. A lifelong struggle is born—between exploration and fear, chaos and confinement. For the first time, we're placed behind bars and incarcerated for the sake of parental anxiety.

Few would argue that parents love their children and wish to keep them out of harm's way. But when fear dominates, childproofing becomes an overriding theme that stunts growth and shouts a constricting message: Curiosity is dangerous! An overabundance of marketing exists to feed this impulse, to the detriment of our children's growth and independence. Consider the huge sums that are spent because of fear; keeping our children "safe" is big business.

A search for "childproof doors" produces more than 59,900 hits. Enter "child proof" and that number balloons to 11 million. It's profitable, this childproofing. Medicine cabinets, kitchen drawers, tops of stairways are all sensible locales for childproofing. Providing barriers to prevent physical harm is one thing.

How many times do we childproof our children by building too much structure into their day, limiting what they can discover *on their own*, correcting them, preparing them to "grow up," until they lose that "utter and complete openness" that is their most exciting trait? We inject *correct* information into them like a vaccine. Afraid they won't discover the *right* stuff, we begin a program of steering their inquisitiveness so they'll behave and be ready for school. Schools take over and begin the program of force-feeding and regurgitation we mislabel *education*. We're missing the point: We don't need to inject, we need to *allow*, because capacity is already there, waiting to be discovered.

> *The word "education" comes from the Latin "educare," meaning to "to lead out," and indicates that the potential intelligence sought already exists within us, and needs to be drawn out. This drawing out by a teacher, system, or environment is the primary function of true education. Thus, talking, for example, is not a skill imposed on a child from without; rather, it develops from an innate capacity encouraged and supported by parents and the youngster's experience of his environment.*[2]

And why do we, as we get older, childproof *ourselves?* We shed our enthusiasm. We reject the words "I don't know," afraid that if we need to keep learning, we haven't learned enough. It doesn't take long for the system to instill the notion that school is merely a stepping-stone toward "real life," a series of assignments we can complete and check off. Graduation is called "commencement," as if it's a beginning that relegates the preceding twelve years to the check-off list. The message: Our learning is over. It's time to get to work!

Rubbish. Keeping our minds open allows us, and those we teach, to rediscover discovery, not as an event, as a way of living. We can continue discovering and continue to be "open to learning for our entire lives," *childlike* in our pursuit of the thrill of the unknown. To do this, we must let go of the complacence that accompanies adulthood. Like our children, like the children around us, we must reacquire the habit of waking to adventure. Not because of what's expected of us, but because of what we can come to expect.

After all, children don't need motivation to learn. They don't get paid for it. They don't even need to get rewarded—they'll practice learning no matter what we do, often in spite of what we do. Sometimes this urge for discovery rubs adults the wrong way, tires us out, so we tell them "Enough! Pipe down! Go play quietly!" Then schools take over, institutionalizing childproofing, ringing bells to march them from cell to cell. What are we protecting children from? (As if they need protection.) Structure begins trumping discovery and control short-circuits the intrinsic motor of exploration.

Some have rebelled. Einstein, Mozart, Newton, Zappa, Clarke, Jobs, Gladwell—all sought the childlike delight of waking to new associations. What about the rest of us? We all arrived on the same train, bent on discovery. Somehow most of us drifted into complacence, or worse, *novelty*, discovery's pale twin. If discovery is our default setting as human beings, something about growing up, about the way we raise and nurture our kids, smothers that natural breath of mindfulness, of noticing fearlessly. Yet that's when we are most human:

> *"Why not send robots?" is a common refrain. And, once more, it is the late Wernher von Braun who comes up with the rejoinder. He often repeated that there is no computerized explorer in the world with more than a tiny fraction of the power of the chemical analog computer known as the human brain, which is easily reproduced by unskilled labor.*[3]

Do we reach our capacity for learning when we don our cap and gown? Do we get full, our brains stretched like bulging balloons? Apparently not. It seems that too much information will not explode our brains. The mathematician John van Neumann has calculated the human brain can store 280 quintillion (280,000,000,000,000,000,000) bits of memory.

That's equivalent to 35 *billion* gigabytes—a nearly limitless hard drive. How's that for discovery? We may have trouble retrieving information, but there is no evidence to suggest our motherboards can achieve overload. Capacity is not the limiting factor, and we can always access the Internet and the cloud for information. Could it be organic, that our brains stop needing new insight? Do they reach some limit of useful learning? As we age, do our brains begin coasting?

Nope. The cells that increase mental connectivity—glial cells, axons, and dendrites—replicate as we make demands on our brains for new connections, no matter our age. Even small adventures, like brushing our teeth or eating with our non-dominant hand, cause these cells to multiply to meet the demand of new chaos introduced into our environment.[4]

So how do we explain why we childproof ourselves and others? We become afraid to question. We're suspicious of curiosity, unable to embrace ambiguity, no longer happy to experiment or to *discover.* It's as though we're inoculated against the *WOW.* What purpose does that immunity serve? When we stop discovering, we stop expanding our capabilities. Worse, we imprison our capacity for insight, the child of curiosity.

The urge for discovery—curiosity—is *a basic human need,* as vital as human touch and love. Anything that twists or restricts that need is unethical. We needn't fear exploration. We no longer slog watchfully through the swamp and climb trees to deny a carnivore its supper. Fear of change is a habit that no longer serves our survival. Further, we needn't allow *discovery* to be suborned by the marketplace as *novelty*—

the childish (rather than childlike), endless, insatiable hunger for *the latest gadget. The newest car. The new season. Same great product in a bold new look. Not sold in stores. Be the first. Limited-time offer. Buy one, get the second free (excluding additional shipping)*, and so on.

Strictly for the sake of profit, this mentality hijacks a basic human need. The grease that lubricates this diversion is a silly, powerful formula: Fast = Easy = Good. There is nothing inherently positive about fast and easy, both of which inhibit learning. Discovery, on the other hand, embraces what John Ciardi aptly named "the pleasure of taking pains."[5]

When we accept that *easy* is the opposite of *hard* (it's actually the opposite of *interesting*), and that *play* is the opposite of *work* (it's actually the opposite of *ignorance*), we buy junk we soon discard. Manufacturers sell products by shortcutting this primary motive to discover. They substitute novelty for discovery, and imply that it is essential. Soon we stop searching and start expecting. We act childish instead of childlike. Eventually we grow childproof, protected from wonder because we don't have time to discover since we're moving on to the next thing. Unlike the urge for novelty, *wonder* can take its time through the process of discovery. Every teacher, every parent, every trainer has a primary responsibility: the reintroduction of wonder. It matters not if the participants are six or sixty. It's not easy. It is *simple*:

1. Trust the motor of curiosity.
2. Use chaos.
3. Reverse the funnel.

Trust yourself and those around you enough to *encourage* uncertainty. Discovery waits eagerly to unspool. All it needs is the catalyst of possibility. Only our own doubts and fears limit our capacity as leaders of learning, whether we're teachers, trainers, or facilitators. We can unleash discovery in the classroom, but we can't control it. Learners need to embrace trust and fearlessness. They have little reason to if their learning leaders—parents, teachers, trainers, and professors—control and guide with an iron hand. That iron hand communicates distrust and anxiety. Teaching is, after all, *marketing*. In its purest sense, that means the marketing of frameworks, context, and ideas, not the imposition of a point of view. When we model fearlessness by relinquishing control, we announce: "I don't need to be sure where this will lead; I'm simply certain that curiosity always serves us well." As Ben Zander, conductor of the Boston Philharmonic, simply and eloquently puts it:

> *It is a characteristic of a leader that he never doubts the capacity of the people he leads to fulfill whatever he is dreaming for them.*[6]

I was surprised by this approach when, as a junior at Washington and Lee University, I signed up for a class in Jacobean drama. I had taken several classes from George Ray, my favorite English teacher. We'd covered all of Shakespeare and survived a whirlwind Modern Drama class (nicknamed "A Play a Day with Ray").

Ten students assembled nervously in a small room. We sat around a table instead of in traditional rows. I felt uncomfortable. After checking the roll, Dr. Ray said, "Each of you is responsible for teaching two plays to the group." I gulped. I knew nothing of these plays. Hey, isn't he paid to teach us? I couldn't comprehend that the ignorant would teach the class. I felt betrayed. My favorite teacher was copping out. Then I started learning. I would wake up in the middle of the night to scribble questions about "my" plays. The experience was frustrating, scary … and exciting.

Forty years later I can still visualize every scene of Marlowe's *Tamburlaine the Great* and Ben Jonson's *Volpone*. Why? Because *I learned without being taught*. Dr. Ray gave me a huge gift and lifelong insight that has served me well. While my first impression had been that my teacher was a goof-off, in time the opposite revealed itself. He took his responsibility seriously enough to back off. I've never forgotten his best lesson: *Teaching takes less courage than allowing learning*.

In the work I do with adults, often mislabeled "training," I need to remind myself every day that *it's up to them*. I need to remain fearless and trusting whenever I have the privilege of presenting myself as a leader of learning. If I embrace one commandment/lesson/mantra, it is *Encourage Chaos*.

When uncertain, we often fall back on imposing order to "straighten out" the learning environment, to right the ship. But wait, the ship isn't sinking. It's only heeling under the pressure of the winds of discovery, as sailboats are designed to do. We may be tempted to back away from the breeze and turn on the engine to show who's in charge. It's noisy with the engine running, and at least it feels like control! Predictability feels like safety. Back to the harbor with some tame lessons we go.

To maintain control in the classroom (while appearing to be open to exploration), traditionalists focus on puzzles, solvable with additional information instead of mysteries, which, like the wind, lack predictable direction. Puzzles (quizzes or closed questions such as, "Does anyone know …?") may titillate and lead to important information; on the other hand, they tend toward tameness rather than wickedness[7] because there is a closed set of answers—usually a very small set: one.

Chaos promotes a different level of thinking. Chaos generates mysteries. It takes insight to make sense of mysteries. Insight is developed through experience and expands toward *answers* rather than contracts toward a single answer. Insight can be shared, yet it doesn't stick unless it's generated—and owned—through discovery. And discovery demands chaos. Mysteries encourage diversity and flux. They propagate insight, which leads to the habit of asking questions. This leads to a different expectation. Not The Answer, possibilities.

As teachers and trainers, the chief mistake we make is placing too much faith in our objectives. "By the end of this class, you will be able to …" Sound familiar? Excess control excludes and disallows unplanned learning, and unplanned learning is the stickiest. It stays with us because it arrives unannounced, like the first wave that upends us at the beach. It is the unexpected that engages our most impressive insight.

Try this experiment. List the most important things you learned during your years in school *that still help you make decisions.* I call these *Head Slaps,* also known as Gotcha! Ah-ha! or Duh! moments. Then make a list of what you remember from the classroom syllabus that still helps you make decisions.

How many of the Head Slaps would you guess were part of any course objectives? If you had a terrific teacher, s/he took advantage of the moment's confusion to help you see something. That's very different from planning your learning. We can't plan, but we can invite Head Slaps. We retain what's important to us, what resonates with our developmental journey, our experience, our search, our subconscious, and the random, chaotic quilt of our experience.

So teachers need to get unstuck. They need to let go of this dogged concept of what they're teaching. They need to allow us to ask for their help, and embrace the idea that they may never know (and therefore cannot test) what anyone has learned. Discovery always involves a search for meaning that illuminates experience, delivers a story, connects through context, and develops attachment. Only the learner can do that.

> *Then she returned to her other preoccupation, testing me with the names of relatives and fish and birds from our family tree. I failed miserably. I could think of no reason to remember them, whereas I knew the name of every character I had met in Great Expectations because I had heard them speak. They had shared their thoughts with me, and sometimes as Mr. Watts read aloud I could see their faces. Pip, Miss Havisham and Joe Gargery were more part of my life than my dead relatives, even the people around me.[8]*

Can you see faces of characters in stories you've read, even if you've never seen an illustration or the movie version? Is there any reason to think that your vision is identical to everyone else's vision? If not, then what you took from the story, what you *learned*, is of no less impact because it's different. In fact, uniformity would diminish the lasting change in you that arrived because of resonance. It is deeply personal and, at least from a teacher's view, chaotic. It hits us when we're expanding our search for discovery.

Reverse the funnel by relinquishing control. Focus too tightly on what you're looking for and you'll diminish the opportunities for insight. Upend the funnel: pour ideas out the wide end to avoid focusing toward a single answer. Start with an idea, a conclusion, or a thought, and move toward greater variety. Consider the infinite rather than the finite.

We want answers. It's a peculiarity of the developed brain. So, struggling to understand, we may rely on planning, agendas, subject matter experts (SMEs), rigorous research, and/or tightly controlled conversations. Guided by that set of assumptions, we operate under the apparent safety of boundaries, so we end up knowing more and more about less and less. Why? Because we see an increasingly restricted universe of information. Then we walk away feeling more certain of something we already framed:

> *For the most part, we do not see first and then define, we define and then we see.*[9]

Discovery needs at least a modest dose of chaos to expand into the unknown. Otherwise we operate only within our definitions. Given permission to reach beyond the immediate and to discover, people intuitively know when it's time to listen for agreement. Allowing exploration brings into play more fluid thinking skills: synthesis, intuition, and playfulness. These skills will inform our learning if we pay attention—"That's an interesting idea" is much more useful than "That's right" or "That's wrong."

The three elements that support discovery are *confluent*: they overlap. When we keep these three tools—trust, chaos, and reversing the funnel—at the top of our toolbox and reach for them first, we create an atmosphere of freedom and exploration that shifts the responsibility for learning from the teacher to the student, where it belongs. This is the true democratization of education. Has it occurred yet? Yes, in some places. Does it work? Absolutely.

In 1968 the Sudbury Valley School was founded in Framingham, Massachusetts.

> *They decided to start with nothing and see what made sense. So they discarded ideas that were givens for other schools and came up with the fact that children, like all people, are*

naturally curious and naturally work at all stages of their life
to increase their understanding of the world.[10]

The students and staff at Sudbury schools embrace discovery. I happen to live near a Sudbury school. That is where I saw the excitement and power of assembly, the next chapter of *Learning Chaos*.

———

1. From Patricia Kuhl's "The Linguistic Genius of Babies" (Feb. 2011). Her studies, and others, strongly suggest that babies' brains actually take statistics on phonemes—word sounds—in order to learn language. This ability drops off sharply after one year, and nearly disappears by puberty. Another puzzling and illuminating conclusion is that this brain reaction occurs *in the presence of a live speaker but not in response to a recording or a television.* Her introduction to this fascinating study can be found on TED.

2. Timothy Gallwey, *The Inner Game of Golf,* (Random House, 1981), p. 5.

3. Tom Wolfe, writing about NASA in the *New York Times*: "One Giant Leap to Nowhere." (July 18, 2009).

4. Pointed out by Win Wenger and Richard Poe in *The Einstein Factor* (Prima Publishing, 1995).

5. From *How Does a Poem Mean*, by John Ciardi (Houghton Mifflin Harcourt, 1975). A quick aside: The word "boredom" did not exist until the mid-18th century. Our penchant for novelty and constant stimulation may therefore be a recent behavioral quirk rather than human nature.

6. Rosamund Stone Zander and Benjamin Zander, *The Art of Possibility: Transforming Professional and Personal Life,* (Harvard Business School Press, 2000).

7. The concept of wicked problems began with an article, "Dilemmas in a General Theory of Planning," written by Horst Rittel and Melvin Webber, published in *Policy Sciences* in 1973. A good introduction to the concept can be found at http://www.net-working.com, The Insider, Nov. 2002. In a nutshell, tame problems are well-defined, stable, solved, and done (2 + 2 = 4). Wicked problems morph, vis-à-vis Heisenberg's principle, so each solution produces unpredictable new versions of the problem. Wicked problems demand learning chaos thinking. Wicked problems have no ending rule—they're ponds in which the solution rocks are pitched with crossed fingers and wonder.

8. Walter Lippmann, founder of *The New Republic* (1914), advised Woodrow Wilson and helped start the ill-fated League of Nations. He published seven books, the most well-known being *The Cold War* (1947).

9. From Lloyd Jones in *Mister Pip* (Dial Press, 2006), p. 75.

10. Mimsy Sadofsky on Daria Brezinsky's radio show, "Children Come First," in 2000.

2: ASSEMBLY

Plato + Play-Doh® = Wisdom

In Upper Marlboro, Maryland, just outside of the Washington, DC, beltway, sits a school—two rustic cabins joined by a breezeway. It doesn't look like much, but inside (and outside) there's a lot happening: dozens of children run around, play music, read, research on the Internet, and build things. What's not happening are grades, grade levels, bells, or periods. Students between ages five and nineteen mix with a few adult staff in a noisy operation. Voices, shouts, music, hammering, and running feet on wooden floors provide the sound track. The children and staff work together as equals to operate Fairhaven, a Sudbury school.

I last visited the school in 2005 when my stepson graduated. Although graduation at Fairhaven involves no exams, graduates must assemble and defend a thesis: *Why I'm ready to go out there*. My stepson was among five students who read their theses and their plans for life that day. The struggling student I'd known as a boy had become an articulate, self-assured young man. My stepson assembled *himself* at Fairhaven.

Admission to Fairhaven is easier for the students than for the parents, many of whom require serious deprogramming. Though well-intentioned, Mom and Dad generate most of the problems for the students because of their misfounded assumptions about school and learning. For the kids to prosper, the parents must agree—often grudgingly—to live by a new paradigm:

> *You can't make students learn until they're ready. Once they're ready, you can't stop them.*

During my stepson's years at Fairhaven, my tongue became a mass of scar tissue. Daily, I restrained myself from asking, "Hey, did you do any math, or social studies, or anything other than play, fish, or skateboard today?" I think what preserved my sanity, and probably prevented his meltdown, was dropping him off and picking him up. Fairhaven's a very welcoming place—part camp, part village. And it's completely open. By that I mean there's no physical or emotional sense of separation or division. All the people, large and small, radiate a sense of shared purpose and go about their business with relaxed intensity. It's like a jazz band or improv troupe, where each member fits into a performance they all support. There's no director. The kids create and connect in a self-directed—and self-accountable—community. They argue, friendships fracture, and tears sometimes flow. They battle over decisions and turf like kids everywhere. And they can attend completely to their business, whether playing freeze tag or running the school meeting, because they create and operate the village in which they learn. Every single day. Attendance? Five hours per day is required. Even this can be negotiated for younger students through the Attendance Clerk, a *student*.

Fairhaven's structure is simple:

- The Assembly provides the heart of the school and includes students, parents, and staff. It sets major policy, amends bylaws, sets tuition, makes general budgetary decisions, and awards diplomas, all by majority vote.
- A weekly School Meeting engages students and staff who vote on budgeting, hiring staff, rules, and committees. The Meeting elects Clerks—a Building Maintenance Clerk or a Medical Supplies Clerk, for example—to deal with issues and with outside authorities. Anyone can run for a clerkship. The Meeting is run by an elected Chair and recorded by a Secretary.
- The School Meeting can create Corporations—"groups of members interested in a particular pursuit, who want official recognition from the school in order to be able to raise money for equipment and supplies and to govern the use of certain kinds of equipment and spaces."
- The Judicial Committee (JC) enforces the rules and hears disputes, then decides consequences. It is the only committee on which every student must serve. It refers serious incidents to the School Meeting, which also hears appeals.[1]

Fairhaven is a paradoxical place, a blend of Woodstock and corporate America. At first glance, Fairhaven appears to have no structure. That's not the case—it's about absence of *imposition*—the structure is intrinsic and organic, since all voices engage as much or as little as they want. Everyone at Fairhaven is involved in a dynamic, often unconscious process that moves from cognition (ideas) through design (vision) to assembly (construction). They learn while making. Because they are in charge, students at Fairhaven are always prepared to *act* rather than wait for someone else to act for them. When they need instruction, they ask for it.

A student interested in taking a class, exploring a field of study, or applying to college, works with other students and staff to *make it happen*. Since there are no grade levels, older children often mentor their younger peers. Groups coalesce and reform as interests and friendships develop and change. A team of teenagers may build a half-pipe for skateboarding while another group sets about figuring out how to grow tomatoes for a pizza project, and a third group researches Mesozoic amphibians because they want to design a computer game using dinosaurs. Most of them go to college. At the age of 14, two of my stepson's friends enrolled in classes at the local community college.

While my stepson attended Fairhaven—or maybe attended *to* Fairhaven—I was employed as a resource teacher in a public school system. I worked in every elementary school in the county. The contrast with Fairhaven was surreal. While some of the schools I worked in were more strictly run than others, none allowed the students to DO very much. The kids trooped about the halls in well-ordered formations, from event to event, while teachers admonished, "Let's use our indoor voices, please." In the middle and high schools, students had fleeting moments of freedom tightly bounded by bells and cries of "Get to class!"[2]

Shortly after I left that job, the administration cancelled recess, the do-somethingest (and in my mind, the most valuable) part of the school day. Why the change? Administrators decided the students needed more time to get ready for standardized tests.

Do you remember recess? Air, sun, giggles and screams, games, tag, escape! Sitting in chairs for hours on end is terrible for us physically.[3] Restless leg syndrome doesn't flare up on a hike. And *restless mind syndrome* doesn't flare up during recess. In time, butt-bound students gain butt-bound minds. Do we learn while seated in class? Of course. I was a good student, got good grades, and good SAT scores. Here are some of the skills I learned while butt-bound in class:

- How to look interested. Very important skill for meetings and family reunions.
- How to look busy. Ditto.
- How to use a toothpick crossbow. (My brother and I invented these. Small enough to carry in a shirt pocket, the tiny arrows were fletched with corners we cut off the file cards intended for term-paper research. The bows were very accurate and nearly silent. I wonder if our toothpick arrows are still embedded in the cafeteria ceiling at Central Bucks High School.)
- How to whistle through your nose. I never did master this. I had a friend who did. Teachers pulled out their hair trying to locate the culprit producing this eerie, piercing sound. Maybe I'll take lessons. I could use this on the subway.

During recess we don't have to look interested, because we are. Recess lets us learn about friendship, self-direction, teamwork, and critical thinking—games. Think about it. When do we get to play the most games at school? Recess. That marriage between critical thinking and doing seldom happens in class.

In my work with adults, whether they're new employees, rising managers, or senior executives, I warn them up front that we're going to be engaged. They are going to do everything we discuss. I don't call the activities "games" because that word may be enough to curtail participation. But that's really what they're doing. They receive a problem, a puzzle with lots of ambiguity. There is no single answer. The content we have covered is all fodder to cultivate a solution. All they need, they brought with them or gained in the course. They work in groups, which always produce different solutions. None is right or wrong. Each is a possibility assembled from the participants' individual learning and creativity.

I believe that thinking is most exciting, and most useful, when it is a part of creation, the assembly of something new. Regurgitating information is not. At Fairhaven, I heard the First Amendment cited by a 10-year-old during a student–staff member conflict. They were arguing as equals. Assembling and defending an argument is interesting, a creative act with accompanying excitement and responsibility. Remembering the year Columbus discovered America is not a creative act. Putting things, including ideas, together into creative action powers the history of humankind. Creative action—assembly—should power the classroom as a rule. It should not be reserved strictly for recess.

Assembly connects three metaphors. The brain is a metaphor for thought. Think of the scarecrow in *The Wizard of Oz*, singing, "If I only had a brain." The heart is a metaphor for emotion: "Have a heart …Take heart … Heartbroken." The hand is a metaphor for assembly: "Hand-picked berries. Hand-crafted baskets." Of the three, the hand metaphor gets the most mileage (and the least respect):

Put our hands together = appreciation
Hands-on = practical
Give me a hand = assistance
Many hands make light work = collaboration
Hands across the water = international cooperation

Erector sets, Lincoln Logs®, sandcastles, appliance-box forts, Sim City®, playing a musical instrument, writing and rehearsing a play—all are intellectually challenging. Of greater significance, they all involve design and assembly. Taking a standardized test does not. Even the most challenging tests, where students have to use critical thinking, don't involve building something. Involvement is what makes learning stick. Children and adults need to build with their minds *and* their hands. Sudbury schools provide this integration, and others are starting to catch on. In a Learning Chaos environment, study (research, planning, design) works well when combined with the best elements of recess (play, fun, creation). It works because of assembly. And that's not merely theory, it's *practice*:

1. Build something.
2. Lessons lead to a product.
3. Handy Brains.

Building the Helmet

The Toshiba/National Science Teachers Association sponsors the ExploraVision Awards every year, the largest competition of its kind for grades K–12 in the hemisphere. Students from the United States and Canada assemble thousands of projects in the fields of science and technology.

Four fifth- and sixth-grade students from Herndon, Virginia, swept their age category in 2011. Each won a $10,000 U.S. Savings Bond. Their winning entry? The *Heads Up!* helmet, designed to minimize soldiers' head injuries. "When you work together you can come up with more productive ideas faster and a lot easier," noted Sydney Dayyani, 11, "and it makes it more fun."

Sydney attended a middle school, two of the other prize winners attended an elementary school, and the fourth was a homeschooler who attended the Virginia Virtual Academy of Herndon, the team's sponsor. They began the project after reading an article about a soldier who had suffered severe head trauma. Together they researched magazines, books, and the Internet, then overlapped sheets of high-impact plastic around temperature and air sensors and incorporated bullet-stopping gels to build a prototype. You can see their design and more information on helmets at the website they designed: dev.nsta.org/evwebs/30n. The students hope that someday their design will be used in the manufacture of improved helmets. As Jovia Ho, 11, observes, "Military helmets needed to be improved because bullets are made stronger now, and bombs are stronger."[4]

Building: The Dome Contest

In June of 2012 four teams of fourth graders in Beaver Dam, Wisconsin, rolled 975 sheets of the *Beaver Dam Daily Citizen* into 195 "logs." They connected the logs with 312 machines screws, washers, and wing nuts to create 4' x 8' geodesic domes. Lifting the completed domes, they raced to the finish line in Prairie View Elementary School's multipurpose room.

Jesse Peters, Prairie View's principal, noticed the students' focus on competing without belittling the other teams: "The geodome competition is a great opportunity for students to learn introductory building and design principles in a fun, cooperative setting."

"While watching the competition I was impressed with the behavior of the Scary Fairies team that was the first to arrive at the finish line," said Marge Jorgensen, the local board of education president. "They did not gloat about being first, but chose to cheer on their classmates."

The contest engages students in a competitive yet "collegiate" application of scientific and engineering principles, communicating, project management, and collaboration. Like most active learning, it opens up areas of engagement for self-direction and excitement.

If you visit Beaver Dam, you'll find the winning dome hanging in Kornely's Craft & Hobby Center, over the cashier's counter.[5]

Lessons and Product: "Dream Garage"

Science labs, field trips, hands-on empirical experimentation are rare in rural areas and poor neighborhoods. These activities often fall victim to the budget ax. Sometimes kids visit the zoo or a planetarium, or a hands-on discovery center. That's too often the exception. Usually, science comes at them from a book or the Internet. Dan Sudran decided to take kids into the lab through a program called Community Science Workshop Network, which helps fund six science workshops in low-income areas throughout California. Each is affectionately known as "The Dream Garage."

Dan grew up in Kansas City, and went to college and law school. "I couldn't really figure out what I was or what I was supposed to be," he says. "I didn't go to college because I wanted to. I went because that's what you were supposed to do." Science bored him. As he closed on 40, he began tinkering with electronics and collecting bones and fossils.

"My life is immeasurably better since I got into science," Sudran says. He discovered this love not from school but outside of it.

Greenfield, a small farm town that is mostly Hispanic, lies about 140 miles southeast of San Francisco. In Greenfield City Hall, Sudran established a science lab—a living, and lively, experiment, not a museum—filled with equipment, power tools, bones, a turtle, and a snake. No classes or curriculum, no tests, no seating charts, lots of action and lots of noise. Kids are busy examining tadpoles, building an underwater robot, and designing a hot-air balloon.

"It's your own dream garage, in a sense," Sudran says. "Just a bunch of stuff you can play around with, without being nervous that the curator's gonna have a nervous breakdown. There are no curators."[6]

Test Scores (Lessons) and Greenness (Product)

One hundred and eight schools from 28 states have discovered a surprising perk to active environmental programs: better test scores. In a study published by three researchers from the University of Colorado's Department of Geography and Environmental Sciences, these schools show a strong correlation between vigorous environmental programs and improved science achievement scores.

"When you have all these together (strong curriculum, stewardship, and service learning) in a school and you use that as your medium to help students learn and to help teachers learn," Bryan Wee, an associate professor at CU Denver, says, "I think you do get a sense that students learn better, learn the content better."

Along with Hillary Mason and Jason Abdilla, fellow researchers at CU, Wee was careful in his conclusions. The three agreed the study is inconclusive that the schools' environmental programs produced the better scores. But they suspect that the culture of the schools—stressing active environmental stewardship—correlated with an increased interest in science that focused attention, with better scores. "School culture really permeates the entire school. When students get a sense of ownership of their learning, when they can connect it with what they're experiencing at home, having a school mission, a very explicit statement about who we are, what we are about, certainly can support student learning."

The team is pursuing more research to clarify the relationship between the schools' culture and academic achievement. "The more research we can do in these areas substantiates the evidence," says Wee.[7]

Mileage (Product) and Grades (Lessons)

Supermileage Vehicle Club is a one-credit course offered every fall at Edgerton High School, where students design and construct at least one operating gasoline-powered vehicle. They have done so since 2009. In 2012, with some new ideas and design changes, Wisconsin teenagers in the class designed two cars they hope will surpass last year's model. Their three-wheeled vehicle achieved 160 miles per gallon. Each year they build on the experience of previous prototypes.

"We're really, really excited to see how both vehicles will run, especially the new one," says Max Ylvisaker, the team's captain. In the spring, they'll compete in two contests sponsored by the Wisconsin Energy Efficient Vehicle Association. "I tell the students that I need a vehicle to get me from point A to point B safely and efficiently," says Joe Mink, who teaches technology at the school and helps the students. "The tough part is actually doing it."

The students not only design and build the cars, they also solicit funding through private donations of hardware, money, and materials.

As Mink says, "The club requires students to use math and science, but even English comes into play." Many club members go on to seek careers in engineering.[8]

When schools weave study and assembly together, students become focused and energized. The more we trust students to *do it*, the *more* they will *do*; and they'll find the way. In such situations, a teacher becomes a referee and a resource rather than the supervisor. We don't need to make kids do things, just *let them do things*. This isn't strictly kid stuff, either. Adults love recess, too.

At the University of Chicago, for four days every May, a couple hundred students participate in the annual Scavenger Hunt. The University of Chicago has produced an impressive number of Nobel Laureates and is famous for student-designed T-shirts making fun of the school's reputation as a nerd farm, among other things.

Started in 1987, the Scavenger Hunt activities have included:

- Unboil an egg;
- Break the sound barrier with a potato;
- Fabricate a working nuclear reactor (actually completed in a dorm room);
- Build a laptop charger using only materials available in the 16th century;
- Revamp a Xerox® machine for office warfare;
- Design a Scrabble® game consisting of nonexistent words, for which the players must provide definitions.

The winner receives a magnificent prize of $300.[9] Perhaps these soon-to-be-working adults are having a last childhood fling. Or, perhaps we need to encourage more of this kind of creativity as a valuable part of being an adult. Why brand it as something to leave on the playground?

How about Tinkering 101 as a prerequisite for all college classes as a way to prep students for making something?

Now let's turn to grown-ups. A few years ago, during a session I facilitated on Critical Thinking, one of the participants mentioned a fellow named Robert Rasmussen, telling me I had to "check him out." I wrote the name down and promptly lost the paper. The following year, the name popped up in a leadership chat group. I Skyped Robert in Denmark, where he lives. In no time we discovered our shared interest in learning and play. Soft-spoken and thoughtful, Robert provides training using LEGO® SERIOUS PLAY®.

Using the Lego pieces, people "think through their fingers," Rasmussen says, "revealing aspects and relationships, some already known, some unknown, focused on their organization." Because the elements of assembly and play are in effect, they can embrace storytelling, possibilities, and candor to generate powerful insights. By talking about the model, the "physical and tangible construction allows for you to have conversations to flow without the fear of treading on personal feelings."[10]

The sessions are active, tactile, and provide a safe language—the bricks. Using them opens a new and neutral dialogue about perceptions, and fosters a shared vision for what is and what might be. The construction belongs to the participants, and they collaborate on the assemblage. Like a Fairhaven School for professionals.

These examples capture the impact of assembly—people engaged in what some might call OJT (on-the-job training). They're excited, involved, and focused on *making something*. That's the piece that's so critically absent in public schools as well as in the office. Somewhere we lost respect for the architecture of integrated learning: hands and mind together. We disintegrated the wholeness of physical learning and demoted the hands to second-class citizens. That dysfunction is a reflection of an unfortunate arrogance about the value of manual work.

"Got a wife, got a family, earn my living with my hands" begins Randy Newman's song, "Birmingham."[11] In that opening he captures a broken premise in education and in our culture. We divide work, schools, even communities, into two camps. That division builds walls between collaboration, understanding, and robust learning. In many ways, this separation is more corrosive than gender, race, or age. It's a dangerous division that falsely detaches "academic" from "manual arts" tracks, white- and blue-collar employees, management and labor, suits and dungarees.

From that division comes "working class" as a supposed indicator of limited intellectual ability. So, managers mouth phrases like "roll up our sleeves and get our hands dirty" *only as a metaphor.* While we admire "handmade" and "handiwork" from a distance, we socially and intellectually denigrate working with our hands. A prime example? Gardening. It's spawned countless books, magazines, and suburban clubs as a hobby. To a subculture of immigrants, gardening is work. A livelihood. People boast about their gardens at cocktail parties. They would be hard-pressed to brag about tending someone else's for pay.

We admire tennis players, pianists, painters, sculptors, and violinists. Many of them achieve fame and, sometimes, fortune, using their hands. They train for years, even decades, to master what we label "hand-eye coordination." It's really *hand-brain* coordination. Ample research exists on the special engagement of the brain in assembly, as opposed to sitting and thinking. Even working on a computer, which is a physical act, provides only a limited learning engagement. Just because we don't swing axes doesn't mean we can't connect learning to assembly.

Haptics, Limerance, and Proprioception (Handy Brains)

Some people blame technology for poor student achievement. Others see technology as the panacea for classroom boredom. Technology only magnifies the impact of poor curriculum and is neither the hero nor the villain. My computer keyboard is an extension of my hands and mind. So is my soprano saxophone, an electric drill, and a Japanese pull saw. Even a television requires tactile connection through the remote. All of these serve as extensions of our hands and our minds, but they're different neurologically, and they're different in terms of the learning that takes place from repetition and from the quality of the connection. The students who built the helmet and the fuel-efficient car used computers. They also used their hands and made something tangible. Their excitement grew from both.

Our schools separate history class from shop class and that's a mistake. It's not opposition to technology that I'm advocating.[12] We need to mix it up in the classroom, to vary what students do and how they do it. More and more research supports the idea that different kinds of learning—brain operation—take place through different media and through different levels of engagement. Creating something *tangible* is a special kind of engagement, be it a geodesic dome or an entire school. Be it with a saw or a 3-D printer.

Professor Anne Mangen studies haptics at the University of Stavanger in Norway. Haptics "refers to the process of touching and the way in which we communicate by touch, particularly by using our fingers and hands to explore our surroundings."[13]

In one experiment, she worked with two groups of adults given the task of learning to write in an unknown language. One group used keyboards. The other wrote the old-fashioned way—by hand. Those who wrote by hand consistently outperformed the keyboard group. Scans revealed that the Broca's area in the brain—linked to language generation and understanding—was more strongly active in the handwriting group. "Our bodies are designed to interact with the world which surrounds us. We are living creatures, geared toward using physical objects—be it a book, a keyboard or a pen—to perform certain tasks," she writes.[14]

Watch people at play and it's obvious that the physical part of learning is immensely important. The implication that working with our hands is somehow less than working with our brains is not only arrogant, it's untrue. It denies congruence and it denies integration. There's even a term for the creative integration of the inner (thought) and outer (physical) lives: *Limerance.*

> *The desire for limerance drives us to seek perfection in our crafts. Sometimes, when we are absorbed in some task, the skull barrier begins to disappear. An expert rider feels at one with the rhythms of the horse she is riding. A carpenter merges with the tool in his hand. A mathematician loses herself in the problem she is solving. In these sublime moments, internal and external patterns are meshing and flow is achieved.*[15]

The power of *flow* is also celebrated in the work of Mihály Csíkszentmihályi, the director of the Quality of Life Research Center, a nonprofit research institute that studies human strengths such as optimism, creativity, intrinsic motivation, and responsibility. He suggests that the "flow state is more likely to appear, and more likely to be powerful, when cognition and proprioception combine."[16] *Proprioception* is the feedback loop that tells our body what to do and reminds us what our body is doing.

The connection between thinking and doing—assembly—is even more strongly underscored by the work of Frank Wilson. He advocates that the brain evolved to manage the complex operation of the hand, *rather than the other way around.* He proposes that the astonishing complexity of the hand "permitted humans to become, at once, both the most delicate and the most dangerous of the primates."[17] Even if your natural skepticism (more on that later) leads you to dismiss Mr. Wilson's contention, there is no organ in nature, or a part of any known creature, that can replicate the range of utility of the human hand, the tool of *assembly.* Disengagement from making something tangible may, therefore, disengage the brain from making the necessary connections we call *learning.*

As I read *The Hand: How Its Use Shapes the Brain, Language, and Human Culture,* it unlocked a flood of memories about things I learned to do, things I still love to do, that spring from my hands. Playing the saxophone, the guitar, and the mandolin. I finger-pick the stringed instruments. A flat pick frustrates my hand. It constrains my fingers. They're much more useful (and happier) operating individually. Woodworking. Sailing. Kayaking. Cooking. All integrate the mind and the hands.

Unable to sleep after a couple chapters of *The Hand* one night, getting on my own nerves, I realized I needed to stop thinking about the book and make something. I sketched a chart along a baseline involving thought ("Cognition") and physicality ("Proprioception"). The left side of the chart involves behaviors where *the hand serves the brain* and the results are primarily conceptual. The right side of the chart involves behaviors where the *brain serves the hand.* Not surprisingly, the results tend toward action and touch. Neither side is exclusive. Every thought involves physical acts and vice versa, even automatic acts as simple as breathing. Clearly, some activities are predominantly one or the other, some both. Where schools miss the boat is in precluding a healthy dose of the right-hand column. The divorce of the hands from learning even has its own dark word: detachment.

I suggest that a Learning Chaos environment generates a healthier balance between thought and activity than the traditional school environment, where thinking has more credibility as a higher-level behavior than making something tangible. I had great fun making the chart, much more than if I'd simply thought, or even just written, about it. This useful distinction helps me keep my own learning balanced when I get thought-bound and forget to *do*. As Ben Zander says, "Once a distinction is made, you have it for the rest of your life."[18] So here are some distinctions.

The Chart

Cognition ←   → Proprioception

Reading an ebook   Reading a book
Power Boating   Sailing
Setting up a golf shot   Hitting a golf ball
Waking thoughts   Dreaming
Speaking   Whispering   Singing   Yawning
Bowling   Juggling
Taking a standardized test   Building a diorama
Reading a recipe   Cooking   Eating   Chewing
Painting
Sculpting
Woodworking
Writing a song   Playing a song
Using power tools   Using hand tools
Finger painting!

As soon as *finger painting* came to mind, a sensory memory clobbered me. I could feel the moisture on my fingers and the textured paper, I could smell the paint. The grip of that memory reinforces the staying power of assembly—what coaches call *muscle memory*—a deep and abiding learning that stems from guided physical repetition. Even Einstein, in his diary, credited "muscular sensations" for many of his breakthrough insights.

Finger painting provides a useful metaphor for Learning Chaos, just as "Paint by Number" does for traditional education. The first is the most tactile and sensuous plastic art that most of us ever experience. The second creates a copy designed by someone else.

There's an unfortunate tendency to play it safe in our schools, to be suspicious of painting outside the lines, much less *without* lines. The photographer Dewitt Jones suggests, "It's not trespassing to go beyond your own boundaries." And it's *our* boundaries that limit students, not theirs. We, as parents, teachers, and trainers, need to trust that children can run the show with *much less* instruction from us. Let them *ask* as part of their development. The same goes for adults in organizations. Trust them to learn from creating rather than from replicating. Trust them to ask for instruction when they need it, not when we need to give it.

Every day's lesson should produce something. It can be as tangible as a high-mileage car or a geodesic dome, as small as rearranging the classroom for the next day's work or sharing a drawing that captures the *aha* about two thoughts colliding.

Learning Chaos starts with the embracing of discovery, the habit of loving ambiguous possibilities. From there, assembly provides a product. Because making something reinforces the value of discovery: *we figured something out*, and *here's what we made*. Those two acts create a community of involvement, a sharing of points of view. The added bonus is we learn from this hands-on process that *you* see things differently from *me*—and that adds to what we do. We open the door for insight and production when we practice wondering, about ourselves and about others. That's skepticism, the next chapter.

———∞∞∞———

1. All the material in this bulleted section is taken from Fairhaven's website.

2. In 2011 a middle school outside Washington, DC, labeled all hallways on their school maps "behavior transitional corridors."

3. A quick (and entertaining) read on this is "Confirmed: He Who Sits the Most Dies the Soonest," in *The Atlantic*, Aug. 22, 2012. It references some more technical information about the hazards of sitting, from the *Archives of Internal Medicine*.

4. Margaret Webb Pressler, *The Washington Post*, May 24, 2011.

5. David Genereaux, "Special to the Citizen," from the *Beaver Dam Daily Citizen*, June 13, 2012.

6. Excerpted from an interview on KQED, June 21, 2012.

7. Taken from a transcript of "When Schools Practice Being Green," written by Nelson Garcia for *9 News.com* in Denver, CO.

8. Dan Lassiter, Associated Press, in *Kidspost, The Washington Post*, June 23, 2012.

9. Excerpted from Patricia Marx, "The Hunter Games," in *The New Yorker*, July 2, 2012.

10. All quoted sections are taken *verbatim* from the LEGO® SERIOUS PLAY® website.

11. Warner/Chappell Music holds the copyright, from the album *Good Ole Boys*, 1974.

12. Displaced workers in 19th-century England invented King Ludd, who replaced Robin Hood in the early 19th century as a hero of the downtrodden. Like Robin, he lived in Sherwood Forest. He was the imaginary leader of a real movement, the Luddites, named for Ned Ludd, who destroyed some mechanical stocking frames around 1785. Today there's a movement called the *neo-Luddites*, a group that eschews technology. I'm neither a Luddite nor a neo-Luddite. When I propose working more with our hands, I'm not suggesting we smash our electronics and dig latrines.

13. Richard Alleyne, "Write it don't type it if you want knowledge to stick," *The Telegraph*, Jan. 20, 2011.

14. From *Front Page News* at the University of Stavanger website, translated by Astri Sivertsen, June 27, 2012.

15. David Brooks, *The Social Animal*, (Random House, 2011), pp. 208–209.

16. Mihály Csíkszentmihályi, "Optimal Experience in Work and Leisure," in *Journal of Personality and Social Psychology, 1989*, Vol. 56, No. 5, 815–822. The article was coauthored by Judith LeFevre. Researchers at the Brain Science Institute in Japan have also provided insight into the idea of optimal experience when studying Shogi players. Shogi is similar to chess, and Dr. Xiaohong Wan and his colleagues at the Institute have found that experts at the game have differently wired brains than amateurs, the implication being that their physical repetition of play created a condition where learning accessed different parts of the brain and created increased aptitude.

17. Frank R. Wilson, *The Hand: How Its Use Shapes the Brain, Language, and Human Culture.* (Vintage Books, 1998), p. 102.

18. Wilson, *Hand*.

3: SKEPTICISM

Don't believe everything you think.

—(Bumper sticker)

Skepticism: the attitude your parents warned you about. Discovery and assembly, the first two elements of Learning Chaos, seem benign enough. Recall the cars, the dome, and Sudbury schools in the previous chapter. We enjoy exploring new ideas and making things. It's in our nature. We learn and create wherever we are—in or out of the classroom. Nothing impedes our natural curiosity—until we go to school. It wouldn't take much for schools to encourage more discovery and assembly. They could start by making room for behavior we already know and like.

Skepticism is another story. Schools don't encourage skepticism because it flies in the face of the conventional. It creates ambiguity. That's a no-no. Why? Because schools focus on control—hall monitors, school boards, periods and bells, detention, standardized tests. Skepticism's payoff is neither immediate nor comforting. Skepticism is a troublemaker, generating waves and upending assumptions. Perhaps most alarming to administrators and educators, skepticism challenges dogma and authority.

Skepticism chafes. It confronts our assumptions and our comfort with habits—especially habits of thought. It provides the antidote to complacency. Rooted in a philosophy based in rigorous questioning as the best method for attaining truth, skepticism is a relatively reasonable stance.[1] In a Learning Chaos environment, skepticism keeps us focused on what others say, but more important, on what we say. *Is that a fact or an opinion? How do I know? How have my beliefs colored what I just heard? What can we agree on? Why do I have to be right?* Skepticism, like charity, begins at home, and questions our tendency to push *our truth* as *THE TRUTH.* Practicing skepticism is no more harmful than practicing respect. Its name has been besmirched. In the words of the 39th vice president of the United States, Spiro Agnew—who could have benefited mightily from a dose of skepticism—it has become associated with "the nattering nabobs of negativism."

Skepticism is not negative. Nor is it sarcasm or naysaying. And it's definitely not cynicism. Skepticism *inoculates* against cynicism. Cynics push their own attitudes without skepticism and without consideration for others' opinions. Skeptics, on the other hand, are humanists. Skepticism humanizes. It replaces "Since you and I disagree, one of us must be wrong, and it's not me," with "We see this differently." Skepticism encourages listening honestly and openly to everyone, and paying attention without our opinions—usually masquerading as facts—getting in the way. Daniel Moynihan said: "Everyone is entitled to his own opinion, but not his own facts." That encapsulates skepticism, reminding us of our tendency to state assertions as facts. Skepticism is our shield against misunderstanding and fractious debate.

Skepticism helps us see others' beliefs as interesting. It rests on a fundamental truth: *Because I believe something does not mean that other views are wrong.* Considering others' opinions is a strength, not a weakness. In a world changing as rapidly as ours, skepticism is sane behavior. Questioning our assumptions may feel uncomfortable, and it allows us to receive new information and new ideas. To embrace skepticism, we must first become vulnerable. While cynicism encourages apprehension, skepticism demands courage. To struggle with our opinions takes backbone. "It's when we lose our capacity to hold space for these struggles that we become dangerous."[2]

We like feeling certain, especially about our own brilliant opinions. Because our opinions are so precious, we surround them with assumptions. When we come to rest on the "right" answers, those assumptions filter out possibilities. Our schools have the potential of becoming laboratories of informed skepticism—active communities of questions that don't demand answers. We could provide a challenging environment that produces lifelong learners with the courage to question their own crapola. We could engage teachers who see themselves as learners rather than authorities. Students could graduate prepared to challenge ideas and make better decisions—from buying products to choosing a career or a spouse. Yet when it comes to skepticism, the most revolutionary principle of Learning Chaos, our schools drop the ball.

Who are the most egregious ball-droppers? Adults—parents, teachers, and administrators. We may mean well; our training and sense of responsibility get in the way. They promote *conviction.* That sense of *rightness* and *righteousness* evolves into rigidity. What happened? As children, we're happy, energetic, and adaptable, running on the fuel of curiosity. But schools gradually erode that innate curiosity, promoting competition and teaching us to find *the right answer.* Students are increasingly graded on achievement rather than on capacity. At the same time, as we mature we separate into *tribes*. We develop strong loyalties to sports teams, movies, celebrities, cliques, music, clothing, fast-food chains. By the time we're adults, we're *certain! If you're not one of US, you're one of THEM.* Attitudes assemble a plow that sweeps over or around conflicting ideas. The result? Stating positions without considering options becomes an infectious habit of absolutes. Skepticism is the vaccination that prevents this from erupting.

> *"There aren't any absolutes. Life would be simpler if there were, but it doesn't work that way."*
> *"Now I've got you, Old Man."* She said it with a certain disputational fervor. *"There are things we know for certain."*
> *"Oh? Name one."*
> *"The sun's going to come up tomorrow morning."*
> *"Why?"*
> *"It always has."*
> *"Does that mean that it always will?"*
> *A faint look of consternation crossed her face. "It will, won't it?"*
> *"Probably, but we can't be absolutely certain. Once you've decided that something's absolutely true, you've closed your mind on it, and a closed mind doesn't go anywhere. Question everything. That's what education's all about."*[3]

To survive, skepticism (open-mindedness) has to swim against two powerful currents. The first is internal. We like to be right. No, we love to be right. If that means you are wrong, so be it. To protect ourselves from the slightest possibility of being wrong, we listen selectively. Right people—those who agree with us—say the right things. Wrong people—the intransigent fools on the other side—say the wrong things. And who would want to listen to wrong things, I mean, really? Because we filter information without questioning—the opposite of skepticism—we hear and see things that support us. Biased assimilation is not the name of a techno-rock group, but the tendency of people to give weight to information that supports what THEY already think and to dismiss information that contradicts it.[4] It's also called a *self-fulfilling prophecy, confirmation bias, right-mindedness,* and *brilliance.* The stronger the position, the more we look up to the decisive speaker.

We admire decisiveness. We look down on waffling. We equate ambiguity with weakness. The quarterback who can't make up his mind gets sacked. So does the indecisive executive. This certainty drowns out skepticism. What takes its place is a comforting habit as we mistake certainty for legitimacy: "If you don't believe in something, you'll fall for anything."[5] Hogwash. Being too quick to believe in something *without question* is what causes human disaster: Nazi Germany, Jonestown, racism, intolerance of any kind. All forms of groupthink are powered by unquestioned allegiance and eroded by informed skepticism. Skeptics may be a pain in the ass because they question assertions. On the other hand, they're seldom homicidal. The skeptic is not dogmatically opposed to everything. S/he's not just a naysayer, but someone "who investigates and researches as opposed to him [sic] who asserts and thinks he has found."[6] Think about all the energy, money, and lives that are wasted because we don't ask, *Wait a minute, who says?* Too often, schools encourage compliance when they should promote wave-making. They're bound by administrators and rules—by *authority.*

Authority is the external current that sweeps skeptics aside. Society, too, exerts pressures on us to accept the status quo as gospel and *not* to question. Marketing, politics, media, and development dress up as progress, and celebrity endorsements all do it. Schools could (and should) provide a venue for nurturing the habit of informed skepticism. But too many teachers broadcast: "We know more than you do, and that's why we're in charge. So listen up! Don't question what we say!" Since most kids look up to their teachers, they want to be "like Miss Thomas." Miss (or Mr.) Thomas knows answers, maybe *all the answers*. They are teachers. Like our parents, they know everything. Go ahead, ask them!

We tall people (adults) need to buck the magnet of certainty by not taking ourselves so damn seriously. Lightening up may be the biggest challenge for grownups, especially teachers and administrators, because most people equate seriousness with strength. Even Pyrrho, the first recorded *skeptic*, was a bit fluffed up. It's been said that while out for a stroll, he saw his teacher, head stuck in a ditch. Pyrrho decided there were insufficient grounds for believing it would be beneficial to extricate his teacher. So he kept walking. We don't need to go that far. We can even be skeptical of skeptics.

Teachers, administrators, and parents can encourage healthy skepticism in children—and each other—by being more active regarding their own thinking. As with any growing pains, questioning our assumptions generates discomfort. Over time, if we pay attention, we discover we don't have to *always be right!* We discover that questioning our assumptions is an act of valor, not a symptom of weakness. We find a new respect for clarity of thought rather than absolutes of position. With practice, we can become comfortable with ambiguity. We ask better questions of ourselves and encourage our kids to help us understand different perspectives. We free ourselves from the exhausting effort of sitting in judgment of everyone different. We take ourselves less seriously.

Lack of self-inflation is not a surrender to moral vagary, or ethical quicksand. Our core beliefs are, after all, not negotiable. A lot of opinions are. Food. Movies. Cars. Sports. Clothing. Politics. Let's conserve energy for the important choices and ethical decisions. Let's stop wasting our resources on debating minutiae. As we gain courage, we can listen better to what we say and what we advocate. We can ask ourselves, *honestly*, what have we claimed? What did I hear? Where does it fit on the Skeptical Staircase?

The Skeptical Staircase

Fact

    Theory

        Belief

            Opinion

                Assertion

                    Hypothesis

                        Possibility

                            Intuition

                                Guess

                                    Hogwash

To start, we need to apply the ladder of skepticism to only our own words. Until we take responsibility for practicing self-skepticism, we're merely learning to be cynical and to pick apart others' positions. Bertrand Russell, who penned "On the Value of Scepticism" in 1928, poked fun at himself and coined the phrase "evidence against interest." He spoke of the delight to be found in arguing against our own assumptions and actions by turning over every contrary stone. He suggests skepticism helps to "preserve the lover and the poet without preserving the lunatic."

As we practice, we can become more attuned to language, less likely to butt heads, and more likely to steer toward understanding. As long as we're clear about the words we use when we speak, we can practice learning rather than winning; winning too often focuses on listening for what *we* can use to make *them* lose. When we choose understanding as our goal, we're less likely to lock into positions. We listen differently—for connection. We learn that finding common ground creates more progress than beating down the other person. When we challenge our own thinking, we make space for others to become allies rather than adversaries: *S/he is stating a belief as truth. If I push back against a belief, I'll only encourage defensiveness. Maybe I can move us from belief to possibility so we can listen with less fire. What opinion am I hearing or saying that's stated as a fact?*

Fact is the most abused step on the Skeptical Staircase. Here are the other steps stated as fact:

Belief as fact: Jesus is God's true son.

Opinion as fact: Conservatives look down on poor people.

Assertion as fact: If we elect a liberal president, our enemies will no longer fear us.

Hypothesis as fact: The first Native Americans came across the Alaska land bridge.

Possibility as fact: Intelligence is an evolutionary accident.

Intuition as fact: You're the perfect partner for me.

Guess as fact: Play the odd number and you'll win this time.

Hogwash as fact: Employees are inherently lazy.

Theory is a special category—as close to truth as science can get and the best explanation of observed phenomena (what we can see and touch). The line between theory and fact is tenuous. Treating theories as operational facts helps us to make rational choices so we can combine discovery, assembly, and skepticism within a shared framework. When we assemble a lawnmower, for example, we assume the theory of gravity is, for all intents and purposes, truth.

Gravity, evolution, and climate change are all theories. They meet the test of falsifiability—a rule of logic—because other possibilities may be argued, but the accepted theories are *the best possible explanation of observed phenomena*. If we want to disregard a scientific theory, that's fine. When we label a belief, assertion, or especially, hogwash, as a fact or a theory, we're not serving the cause of learning; we're serving a *cause*. As the great American philosopher, Aaron Neville, said, "Tell it like it is."

Here is a suggestion for practicing the Skeptical Staircase in the classroom. Place jars on a table or on a stepladder. Label the jars with the categories (Assertion, Hypothesis, etc.). Ask students to write down statements they have gathered from the Web, news sources, friends, parents, teachers, administrators, or themselves. Then ask the group to decide which jar should receive each statement. Watch what happens next. Few, if any, of the statements will end up in the *fact* jar. The first gift of skepticism is to distinguish between facts and everything else. Keep the jars on display as a reminder that it's okay to question what *anyone* says. Refer to the jars every day. You might also keep a set at home, in faculty meetings, and on the principal's desk.

In every classroom, we can implement three frameworks that nurture skepticism. They clarify issues, engage students, and activate deep learning.

To nurture skepticism:

1. Break into argument.

2. Beware the equal sign.

3. End with questions.

First, **break into argument**. If this sounds like a contradiction, it's because we have fallen into a misunderstanding through lack of informed skepticism. We often confuse *argue* with *argufy*—a synonym for *wrangle* or *debate*—argument with the intent of winning. The root word *arguer* means "to make clear." We can choose to view argument as a battle. But we need to fight on the same side against the only enemy of learning: ignorance. Arguing should have as its goal an increased understanding of issues and of each other. Working within that framework makes us partners in discovery, rather than adversaries. We don't have to settle anything! If we move toward greater understanding, we've successfully *argued* within the realm of skepticism and Learning Chaos.

Difficult as it may be, we can resist the urge to push back when someone makes a statement. As in t'ai chi or aikido, we can choose to deflect and seek clarity. No aggression required. When we attack, others defend. The vacuum we create by not knocking heads allows those heads to reason together. Every time we converse, we have the chance to be a part of, or apart from, shared understanding. Debate moves us *away* from each other. Listening for clarity (*Is this an assertion, a belief, etc.?*) and entertaining multiple points of view moves us *toward* each other. Unless a perspective is highly objectionable or perverted, this is an opportunity to move toward a handshake rather than a fistfight. Hitting each other, even as a metaphor, serves no one. We need to lose the perception that seeking common ground is a sign of passivity or cowardice. Seeking common understanding shows trust and courage.

The astronomer Raymond Littleton suggests that we imagine a bead on a wire. One end of the wire has a value of zero and is completely false; the other end has a value of one and is absolutely true. He cautions against letting the bead approach either end. In other words, we should beware of too much certainty, allowing events and reason to move the bead back and forth as we find new insights and new information.[7]

Settling into a nonconfrontational mode, we can ask open, neutral questions:

> *What are some possibilities?*
> *What led up to _____?*
> *Can you help me understand what you mean by _____?*
> *How do you see the situation?*
> *What other factors affect this situation?*
> *If you could do anything you wanted, what would it be?*
> *What is the most troublesome part here?*
> *What do you know about it now?*
> *We see this differently; what can we agree on?*
> *How can we find out more about this?*

Once we've grown comfortable with listening for understanding and using neutral questions, we can settle into a *rhythm of argument*. Statements become the basis for reframing—wrapping what was just said into our own understanding and building on it, rather than reacting in a knee-jerk fashion with a counter-idea. Since we don't have to find an answer, we don't have to hurry. Skepticism and arguing, in the Learning Chaos environment, are like breathing. We need the oxygen of understanding *all the time*. We don't breathe with the goal of stopping, so why ask questions with the goal of stopping?

The rhythm of Learning Chaos argument goes something like this: Question Reframe Open Question Agreement New Question

The agreement can be about process (*How can we explore this topic together?*), about our differences (*We grew up seeing this from different angles*), or about how our background and education give us our overlapping—but not identical—perspectives. Any points of agreement will do, as long as we can move forward with a shared goal of confluence—flowing together. Our differences become enriching at this point rather than isolating. This gentle habit of argument keeps us out of the corners, where one of us is wrong and there's only one right answer, and where we lose skepticism in the fog of certainty—foggy because it obscures all other possibilities. That fog of certainty flows from statements that "this is that," spoken as a fact. Such statements are designed to end (win) the argument. In debate it's known as "generating equivalence," a rhetorical trick to create the moment when we can say *Aha! Gotcha!* In a Learning Chaos environment the techniques of debate are useful for sifting through facts and winnowing misleading information; they are not intended as tools for defeating an opposing point of view. So watch out for "facts" spoken as equivalence (_____is_____).

Equivalence: any time someone states that one thing *is* another:

faster is better   biggest is best   efficiency is the answer
young people are lazy   the government is the problem

Whenever a statement implies equivalence, our skepticism alarms should ring. Especially when *we* utter these statements. Try substituting the *equal* sign for *is* or *are* in the above-mentioned statements:

faster = better   biggest = best   efficiency = the answer
young people = lazy   the government = the problem

Beware the equal sign. The equal sign amplifies what these sweeping statements imply—an absolute rightness that falls apart under a little skeptical examination. Tossing these thought grenades may make us feel pithy and wise, like Ben Franklin, but they stifle thought. They're shortcuts. They discourage skepticism. Worse, they preclude learning. Why bother to go through the messy process of asking questions when you can throw a grenade?[8] When we hear a grenade—especially from our own mouths—we need to *question the equal sign*. As an example, take the first one, *faster is better*. Does it apply to children growing up? Developing wrinkles? Eating a delicious meal? Making love? The growth of a tumor? The approaching end of a great book?

How many opportunities for insight, reflection, and connection do we rush past? How often do we put others at risk, emotionally or physically, because we're darting around in our cars? Why do we nudge our children to hurry through childhood, by pushing them to read and master math before they've learned to play for its own sake?

Arguing—Learning Chaos–style arguing—is a powerful answer to equivalence. A simple response to an equal-sign assertion is, *Oh?* We can always push back. Isn't it better to encourage mutual understanding? A series of neutral, open questions leads to a breakdown of the equal sign. When that happens, we have a starting point to engage skepticism and to allow wiggle room for entertaining new points of view. We don't need to contradict. Yes, faster *can be* better. Bigger *can be* better. "Can be" leads us to questions, possibilities, and learning. "Is" does not.

Curbing the habit of simple answers—the equal sign—moves us from blame to consideration. Too often, the equal sign creates villains: Us (the good guys) versus Them (the bad guys). *Them* can refer to supervisors, parents, children, in-laws, neighbors, bankers, lawyers, therapists, Republicans, or Democrats. Equal-sign thinking moves Littleton's bead to one end of the wire. From that perspective, we lose empathy and the need to question. When we're stuck in argufying, the farther away another person's perception is, the farther away their bead sits on the wire, and the *wronger* they must be. When we're stuck in our difference we don't engage and connect, we isolate. Sucked in by the fog of certainty, we stop learning and close down, and our curiosity withers. Learning Chaos says: *The more distant another's perspective is from mine, the more useful it is to help me see what I don't notice from where I stand.* The road to that insight runs through questions rather than answers, no matter how correct the answers may feel.

We can learn to be more comfortable with skeptical thinking when we learn to **end with questions** rather than answers. Whenever we strive toward answers, we usually fall into the trap of *the* right answer. Comforting, empowering, good-grade-getting, and a brick wall. When *the answer*, as opposed to *an answer*, is our goal, learning gets squeezed out. If we frame our thinking, and our learning, toward finding questions, we trust the fire of curiosity. This is not to suggest that answers have no part in Learning Chaos. Facts are useful; they have their place.

Sometimes a narrow question may be satisfied by a narrow answer. *When did Columbus discover America? 1492.* That's factual. The answer can be found through a quick Internet search. It's useful as a starting point to discover and assemble insight about Columbus. But it is not an end in itself. As Pablo Picasso said, "Computers are useless. All they can give us are answers." Students and teachers in Learning Chaos classrooms value computation—when they need *an answer* as the foundation for more questions. Otherwise the conversation is closed, as most exams are closed. Closed answers lead to closed thinking. So, though *1492* is the *correct answer*, it is best used as the starting point for discovery and assembly, rather as an end in itself.

Some examples of "starting point" questions include:

> *Why do we say Columbus discovered America? What about the Vikings in Newfoundland? How about the Portuguese fishermen who took tons of cod off the Grand Banks well before Columbus "sailed the ocean blue"? What happened to the people who were already living in the Western Hemisphere? What did Columbus think he'd discovered? Why did he come in the first place? How big was his ship? Can we make a model of his ship with our chairs? Can we find out what it was like to live in 1492? What did they eat? Why don't we make a sample menu and talk to the cafeteria cooks, then compare their food to ours? How did his discovery change him and his family? Why isn't our country named the United States of Columbus?*

The discomfort of moving from a snippet of information to a galaxy of questions is a small investment in changing how we think. The search for answers is a peculiarity of humankind and an admirable habit. It's a flawed habit when we think the point of the search is ending it. Today, all the information ever known is, for all practical purposes, instantly available. Questions, as a learning habit, can serve as stepping-stones to further questions, with stops along the way for sharing information and arguing toward greater understanding.

Skepticism, in support of discovery and assembly, builds a willingness to listen without judgment. That allows us the opportunity to see all perspectives as valuable, to seek expertise as a resource rather than as an authority, and to engage in learning without fear of constraint—wherever that takes us. In Learning Chaos lingo: fluidity.

1. Pyrrho, *skepticism's* founder, was exceptionally long-lived for his time, 360–270 BC. The commentaries on his life and philosophy chronicle a life that was apparently a montage of Monty Python skits. According to Diogenes Laertius, Pyrrho's chief biographer, he was the originator of the "Doctrine of Incomprehensibility." Wish I'd thought of that. He was reported to have wandered around and talked to himself a lot, claiming that by doing so he was *learning to be good*. If there had been late-night talk shows in his time, he would have been a frequent guest. Or maybe a frequent host on *SNL*.

2. Brené Brown, interviewed by Krista Tippett, *On Being*, WAMA (NPR), Oct. 30, 2012. The topic is her TED talk about vulnerability, which went hugely viral, much to her surprise.

3. David and Leigh Eddings, *Belgarath the Sorcerer*, Del Rey books (an imprint of Ballantine Books), 1995, p. 317.

4. Cass R. Sunstein, *Breaking Up the Echo*, *The New York Times*, Sept. 18, 2012.

5. Ascribed to Alexander Hamilton, Alex Hamilton (different guy), Peter Marshal, Ginger Rogers, and Malcolm X, among others. A fun fluidity exercise—the next chapter—would be to split the class into groups, ask each group to assume the quote came from one of the people mentioned, and ask them to find out enough about that person to suggest what the quote meant in the context of that person's life and times.

6. Miguel de Unamuno, *Essays and Soliloquies*, 1924.

7. Mentioned by Meyer to Travis McGee, two of my favorite skeptics, in *Cinnamon Skin*, by John D. MacDonald, Random House, 1982, p. 272.

8. The grenade-thrower metaphor comes from *Dealing with People You Can't Stand*, by Rick Brinkman and Rick Kirschner, McGraw Hill, 1994.

9. The *Santa Maria* was the largest of the three ships—really small boats—in his expedition. Since she ran aground and was demolished on Christmas Day, the crew apparently passed out, we don't know for sure. Our best guess is she was approximately 58 feet long. That's a few feet longer than the cargo part of a tractor-trailer. She had a crew of 20 and was not designed for an Atlantic crossing, especially since no one in the 15th century knew what body of water they were on.

4: FLUIDITY

It is impossible to step into the same river twice.

—Heraclitus

I once asked him [William Raspberry] how he worked. Did he have some kind of system? Choose his topics in advance? Stockpile "evergreen" columns, unrelated to the day's news, for mornings when inspiration missed its scheduled appointment?

Not really, he replied. He just came into the office, thought for a while and got a sense of what was the right column for that day. Often, he told me, he wasn't quite sure what he thought about the topic until he was well into the writing. I think those were the columns he enjoyed most, because they allowed him to look at his subject from all sides.[1]

—Eugene Robinson

When I was seven, my father showed me how to tie a bowline knot one-handed, without looking. He'd learned the trick from his father.

When I was 11, I needed to pass a knot-tying test for my first Boy Scout merit badge. The assistant scoutmaster sat us down around a campfire and handed each of us a length of clothesline. "Watch carefully," he instructed. "The rabbit goes up through the hole, around the tree, then back down through the hole." I offered to show him my dad's faster way, with no rabbit and no hole. He wasn't interested. I got the merit badge anyway, but I never shook my reputation as a difficult scout.

In 2012, while sailing on the Chesapeake Bay, I showed a friend how to tie a bowline. I had trouble explaining my dad's method, so I tried the rabbit-hole approach. "It's not a rabbit and a hole, it's a pretzel," she corrected me as she tied it quickly. She prefers food metaphors. So here are three approaches for completing the same task: my grandfather's trick, the rabbit, and the pretzel. Is one of them best?

Fluidity, the fourth element of Learning Chaos, suggests there is no best route to understanding. All learning takes place within frames—metaphor (like rabbits and pretzels), story, comparison, analysis, synthesis, contrast, instruction, conversation, argument, inspiration, even desperation. Some of us prefer seeing to understand, some hearing, some doing, in various combinations, never static. A fluid learner, not satisfied with looking at anything through a single lens, shifts frames in order to gain different perspectives. Once we learn to embrace fluid learning, we pay attention to *everything*. Not as a chore, as a childlike practice of openness and excitement: wide-eyed regardless of age and experience. Fluid learning is challenging and sometimes scary, it's never boring. Fluid teachers relinquish the illusion of control that comes with their position. Fluid teachers throw themselves into partnership with their different and equal co-learners—students, other teachers, administrators, and parents. They search for insights rather than end points.

The more fluid we become, the better we can choose, and change, frames. Rules—the most rigid frames—provide a valuable resource with a major drawback: they focus on what has already happened. Fluidity generates possibility because fluidity focuses on what has not yet occurred. In Learning Chaos classrooms, the spotlight shines on expanding capacity rather than on checking off accomplishments. In Learning Chaos classrooms, students grow into flexible learning and explore how to learn as a lifelong habit rather than as preparation for a test.

Students in Learning Chaos settings will be much better prepared for the ambiguity of rapidly changing technology, demographics, and culture. And that habit will serve them well. Whatever the future brings to the professional world, "the demands for new knowledge and skills will be constant, no longer a value-added element, but the essential factor in determining organizational survival."[2] Not only will learning one answer be insufficient, learning one way will be even more so.

Skepticism, the previous chapter, suggests there are many answers. Fluidity suggests there are many pathways. When we cook, for instance, some of us carefully follow recipes and never deviate. Others ask themselves, *I wonder what would happen if...?* The first group relies on predictability: "It worked for Julia Child, so it'll work for me!" Relying solely on directions makes us less flexible. It may be why a dish goes down in flames. When faced with ambiguity, rule-followers may panic. They don't know what to do when a recipe calls for two-thirds of a cup of milk and they only have one-third. A fluid learner is delighted: *I'll try yogurt or sour cream.* Rule-bending in the kitchen leads to new recipes. What difference does it make if they spring from a mistake?

With fluid thinking, when confronted with new information or, God forbid, *a change in plans,* we can expand into possibility. The goal of fluid thinking: curiosity rather than concern. Riveting our efforts to the instructions is *one way* to operate. It's not the only way, and it stifles innovation. If we view recipes—or any instructions—as a beginning rather than the end, we can move forward with our surprises rather than in spite of them.

Fluidity is about learning by *questioning* instructions. Fear of failure—risk—may caution us to follow the tried-and-true methods we were taught. Being bound by habit can be risky business (and not merely as a metaphor, but professionally, as in *business*). What worked yesterday may not be up to the challenges of tomorrow. Instructions serve as a useful pattern for starting, not always for exploring possibilities. "No battle plan survives contact with the enemy," said Helmuth von Moltke. How often do we find our plan rubbing up against messy reality? When we think more fluidly, we spend less time battling ambiguity and more time reaping the benefits of flexibility. The old adage of the five Ps (Prior planning prevents poor performance) implies we can *control what happens.* In chapter one, I made a distinction between planning and preparation. Rule-followers tend to think planning is the key to success. That's a dangerous illusion in an era of accelerating change. Fluid learners know that preparation—keeping our minds open to possibility—is more important than planning. We can prepare to be flexible by practicing fluid thinking. We can't plan *flexibility.*

New environments demand new tools and new methods. When snared by a rigid habit—*this is how it's done*—we don't look for another way, another frame, even if our assumptions aren't working. We try harder instead of backing away and relaxing into new perspectives. Another adage bears true in this case: If a hammer is the only tool you know, every problem looks like a nail. And we won't know how many possible other ways (and other tools) there are until we give them *all* permission to be legitimate.

Which of these two tools looks more like your mental picture of a saw?

If we think *saw*, most of us would visualize the tool on the right. That provides our *frame* for saw. We establish frames based on experience. We think of *elephant* and a picture pops onto our personal computer screen (our mind's eye). These pop-ups are useful shortcuts. They provide a starting place so we don't have to analyze everything from zero. Fluid learners, ever curious, are always expanding their mental models. Childlike, they pay attention and explore new *stuff*. So a fluid learner is less likely to be surprised by a different frame (in this case, a different saw). Fluid learners add the less familiar image to their internal dictionary as another frame, different rather than wrong. They never reject an idea or frame prior to consideration. They don't say, *That's wrong!* They say, *That's different!*

You don't have to be a Rhodes scholar to notice that nearly everything about the saw on the left is the opposite of the saw on the right. Yet it's more efficient and can do additional tasks (such as cutting wooden trim very close to the floor). It uses less steel, has two cutting edges, and more. Our imagination stops at the boundary of our frame … until we get in the habit of fluid learning, a continual expansion of ideas and images. Otherwise, we stop short at our comfortable first thought, a shortcut that excludes all possibilities *outside the frame*. What if you were asked to picture a classroom? Would you see an open field? A planetarium? A kitchen? A school bus? Dreams? Why not? Like the saws, our thinking about teaching and learning starts in a frame that easily becomes a habit. Why? Because we don't question the frame itself.

When traveling, we wonder, *What's the best way to get there?* Ask others, and they'll share their favorite way, usually the shortest, since most people substitute *quickest* for *best*, never asking—and being flexible about—how do you define *best*? If we always seek the shortest route, we miss the illuminating detour. We speak of "getting lost" with embarrassment. What if we saw getting lost as an opportunity *to see things we wouldn't otherwise see and learn things we wouldn't otherwise learn*? Fluid learners are joyfully opportunistic. We don't fear getting lost because that's where we find surprises. Whether we're in a car or grappling with new ideas.

What we learn, over time, counts for less than *how we can continue to learn*. Becoming comfortable with detours gives us access to powerful insights. No syllabus, instructor, or text can make that happen. We discover more—in business terms, greater *return on investment*—when we let open-mindedness and curiosity lead.

In the '70s, when I started teaching, I had to take courses to be recertified. Among them was a state-mandated health course. I was the only male in the class, and six of the eleven women in the class were nuns. Little wonder that at first I was intimidated. Stranger in a strange land indeed!

The teacher happily embraced fluidity, so we were free to gain as much from each other as from the text. I learned a good bit about health—such as diet, the body's various systems, and emotional balance. What was more illuminating, though, and more useful, was learning *how other people very different from me thought about health.* That goal did not appear in the course description, the syllabus, or the objectives. I achieved recertification because I completed the course and, in addition, I became a more mindful and effective teacher by learning through others' eyes. I finally understood that *my students don't think as I think, so they don't learn as I do.* That kind of insight is more likely to occur when the teacher accepts chaos, relinquishing control. In this case, the instructor allowed us to process lessons fluidly. This allowed us to gain insight rather than merely gain information.

Fluid learners don't accept boundaries to learning—in school, after school, instruction, exploration, alone, together. With the added layers provided by the Internet and the cloud, we're growing into a world more ambiguous and inclusive than ever before. We can have real-time conversations with people we have never met and never will meet face to face. So, we can establish learning relationships based on a community without distance. Marshall McLuhan promoted the idea of a global village in *Understanding Media.* He did so in *1967.* He was right then and he's more right now. Thinking globally is not only a political manifesto, it's a mindset, a willingness to *always be ready to reconsider.* In other words, we must be ready to think fluidly. New discoveries and, more important, new insights appear because we accept experience without boundaries.

This may sound intimidating, but perhaps fluidity is no more complex than Francie Dalton and the squirrels. Working with a group of executives, Francie felt frustrated that she could not teach them how to work together (and not take themselves so damn seriously). She went home, poured herself a glass of wine, and *stopped trying to figure it out*. Her eyes were drawn to squirrels "diligently going about their squirrely business." Their persistence, focus, and resourcefulness inspired her to write down 21 characteristics that executives could learn from squirrels. Squirrels, she noted, who are "undaunted that the odds are stacked heavily against them, willing to turn themselves upside down to get what they want, sophisticated communicators, and unconquerably persistent. When confronted by barriers, they find another way to win. They never, Never, *NEVER* give up."

Her closing advice: "If you need to go to work and be a shark, a lion, or a tiger, great." But, she said, when faced with adversity, sharks and other predators attack, while squirrels face each new problem with flexibility. If their first approach (frame) isn't up to the task, they become stubbornly creative. Francie found a terrific metaphor which, like a story, provides the most fluid and abiding lesson. Perhaps it would be more accurate to say that the metaphor *found her*. By allowing room for insight—fluid thinking, and not pushing the frame too hard, she was open to connections she might have otherwise missed.[3] A healthy respect for ambiguity and a willingness to step back and allow answers to find us characterize lifelong learners. What sharks may perceive as a lack of focus is simply openness, an acceptance that learning includes embracing paradox, *reality standing on her head to get attention*.[4]

Sometimes we attribute not learning *enough* to not trying *hard enough*. But trying harder narrows our desire for possibility instead of expanding our intellectual peripheral vision. Given the astonishing speed and capacity of the human brain (particularly the subconscious) to gather and process information, the harder we try, the less successful we may become. Ever try to convince a stubborn child that your way is the right way? As any parent will attest, the harder we push, the more the child resists. A fluid mind is comfortable with the collision of ideas that produces insight, like squirrels and executives, or pretzels and knots. If we're trapped by the concept of learning only within boundaries— subject area, discipline, major—we mistake sweat for study, anxiety for education, testing for learning. The narrower our focus, the less we harness the brain's eagerness for new connections, which is our greatest learning intelligence. As David Brooks suggests, "we are smart because we are capable of fuzzy thinking."[5]

We need to embrace fuzzy thinking, especially in our schools: unplanned exploration deliberately free from conclusions, and far removed from tests. Lateral rather than hierarchical thinking. Why? Because we no longer live in a linear world, if we ever did—*all the easy problems have been solved. From now on, the problems will be tougher.*[6] Tame problems, like balancing our bank accounts, may be difficult, and they're puzzles—they can be solved by information and the application of some fairly straightforward frames. Figuring out gas mileage, choosing a cable service, comparing flight costs, managing everyday tasks, expanding a recipe to feed six rather than two, are all puzzles. Like crosswords, their solution depends on gathering and applying information. For most of these challenges, *the better we are at applying rules, the better we perform.*

However, as problems grow more complex, more *wicked*[7], they exceed the boundaries of puzzles and embrace the realm of mystery. No matter how clever we are, how practiced at applying techniques and rules, we fall short when confronted by the unknown. Mysteries are never solved. They can only be explored. And exploration demands finding new routes. Mysteries demand insight beyond knowledge, comfort with ambiguity, and open-endedness. Raising children, grappling with careers, balancing the demands of modern life, finding contentment, are all mysteries. Whereas fluidity is *helpful* in solving puzzles, it's *necessary* when managing mysteries.[8] So why do we look for a simple answer to complex problems—a political doctrine, self-help book, or a rigid orthodoxy—to solve complex problems?

Two powerful barriers prevent us from thinking more fluidly. The first comes from millennia of focusing on survival. Rigid thinking made sense in a world where new ideas and new information carried threats. *If it's new, it could kill me.* For most of our time on earth, we've focused on a simple set of challenges: Eat, don't get eaten, make more humans. We lived in a world of scarcity. For me to *get*, I must *take*. So we hunted. We invented tools and weapons, and discovered and assembled to protect and procreate. We were skeptical of new ideas. All these behaviors fit into a narrow frame of survival: *If it doesn't help protect us, it's a waste of time.* Any intrusion on our regular habits signaled the *possibility* of a threat. That habit of fearful reactivity may have protected us when we needed protection, when *regular habits* meant *survival*. Many of us still pay lip service to this ancient frame: *Don't rock the boat!*

Even the first brave souls who suggested the Earth was round were greeted with scorn and vilified by rigid thinkers: *Are you insane? We'll slide off!* In the same way, we're trapped by our invested frames when we aren't flexible enough to entertain new ideas. Even worse, when those new ideas come from a new source, such as someone different from us, the threat multiplies. Suspecting new ideas because of an *imagined threat*—a throwback to fear of annihilation by another tribe—isolates us. Isolation, whether from other people or from other peoples' ideas, breeds stale thinking. Opening our mental window is impossible when we live in fear of what might be out there.

So an initial, courageous step in becoming more fluid is to move beyond feeling threatened by what's *new to us*. There are times, even in modern life, when events and phenomena are dangerous. Looking both ways before crossing the street still qualifies as sane behavior. Dark clouds can still presage a dangerous storm. However, many of us hold threat detectors that beep constantly, like the annoying chirp some devices make when their batteries run low. We hear something that chafes against our assumptions. *CHIRP*. Someone disagrees with us. *CHIRP*. A new technology appears. *CHIRP*. Our children push back against our traditions. *CHIRP*. And that *CHIRP* triggers our defenses, immediately stiffening resistance as if we're being attacked.

We can disarm that noise by taking a quick mental breath, back off from reaction, and ask, *Where's the tiger?* What is making us fearful? This gives us the opportunity to steer past a defensive stance, a chance to derail the fight, flight, or freeze response. *We need to defend ourselves only when we're attacked, and a different idea or opinion is an attack only if we make it so.*

The second barrier to fluidity also has to do with struggle, but of a different sort. *If I don't understand, I must not be trying hard enough.* Nonsense. No data suggest that *thinking harder* leads to anything but a headache. It's too easy to fall into the trap of defining learning as struggle: *No pain, no gain. You can't make an omelet without breaking eggs. You got a D because you didn't work hard enough. She's not working up to her ability. He tries hard, and he finds the subject difficult.* I'm not suggesting there's something wrong with hard work; I'm happiest when I'm gnawing at a task. When I need to access understanding, I've learned to walk away, back off, *sleep on it*. The harder I try to think, the less aware I am of connections.

There's even a term for the cost of focusing too tightly: inattention blindness. In a famously viral Internet video, a group of people toss a ball back and forth in a corridor. Some have white shirts, some dark. We're asked to count how many times the white shirts touch the ball. Halfway through the video, a woman in a gorilla suit walks through the group. Half of the viewers *don't see the gorilla*. In another experiment, people were asked to jog behind a volunteer and count the number of times he touched his hat. During the jog, they passed a staged fight where two men were beating up a third. In broad daylight, over 40 percent missed the fight. At night, that jumped to over 65 percent.[9]

When we pay attention too hard, we miss *what we're not looking for*. As a lifelong sailor, I learned early the trick for finding a buoy in poor visibility: *Don't look for it!* Relaxing my eyes and letting them peruse the horizon will invariably lead to discovery. Searching hard leads to frustration and eyestrain. Maybe trying too hard isn't as effective as allowing *play*—both literally and as a metaphor—to kick in. We just need to follow a few gentle guidelines:

1. Admit myopia.
2. Trust lightness.
3. Assume that everyone is qualified.

When we have difficulty seeing objects at a distance, we wear corrective lenses to compensate for our **myopia**. Even those of us with 20/20 vision use binoculars to watch birds, and telescopes to view the stars since we need help to extend what we can *perceive*. As a metaphor, *myopic* applies to thinking. It means *shortsighted*. Just as I may need a nifty long-handled tool with plastic jaws to reach things on high shelves, or a telescoping wand with a suction cup for replacing ceiling lights, I need an *extension* to reach past the limits of my understanding. The issue is not information. We can access a computer for information—we have immediate, practically limitless information via the Internet. We have blogs and chats and tweets and posts. Even with the far reach of the World Wide Web, we're still *myopic*—bound by our mental myopia—because information doesn't add to understanding until we question our frames: *Cada cabeza es un mundo: Each human head is its own world.*

If I accept that my startling brilliance only shines as far as the framework of my assumptions, I've taken the first step toward fluidity. I need to acknowledge, embrace, and celebrate my ignorance. Acknowledge it because *it's true.* Embrace it because it *prompts learning.* Celebrate it because *I'm more fluid when I'm humble.* Our knowledge is finite. Our ignorance is not.

"Ignorance: A Science Course" is actually the title of a seminar for graduate students at Columbia University. Stuart Firestein, chair of the Department of Biological Sciences, teaches the class. He shines with curiosity, enthusiasm, and playfulness. When he started designing the class, he wondered if anyone would sign up and what a grade would mean: "Would students rather get an A or an F in a course titled 'Ignorance'?"

Describing his class, he cites an old adage—*It's hard to find a black cat in a dark room, especially when there's no cat.* He suggests ignorance, not knowledge, is the driver of science: we explore best by admitting that we cannot know the end point. When we buy a puzzle—a jigsaw puzzle, for example—we assume the puzzle has a defined resolution. We may stumble and err, but we know there's a guaranteed solution.

Scientific research is very different, embracing fluidity: *So we really bumble around in the dark. We bump into things. We try and figure out what's what. And then somebody eventually flips a light on, and when we see what was in there, everybody goes, "Oh, my goodness, that's what it looked like." And then it's right on to the next black room, you know, to look for the next black cat that may or may not be there. And science is dotted with black rooms in which there were no black cats.*

Dr. Firestein suggests that even generating a hypothesis involves bias, as we tend to project explanations based on our preconceptions and on what we want to be true. In other words, we are so uneasy with uncertainty that we move too quickly to the comfort of explanation. In our search for the *why*, we produce explanations based on limited understanding. Firestein further suggests we need to grow past the idea that facts are the anchor for knowledge: "We don't know them perfectly, and we don't know them forever. They will change."[10]

History is populated with broken certainties. Some of them, unfortunately, still operate. A surprising number of Americans, for instance, believe that the sun revolves around the Earth.[11] Bogus information that masquerades as truth creates a rigid and dangerous community of certainty as we gather like-minded people around ourselves. That kind of certainty blossoms when skepticism and fluidity are absent, especially in the classroom. When we *admit*—both acknowledge and allow—ignorance, we avoid the dangerous illusion that we know *everything we need to know*. That's simply never the case, no matter how experienced, erudite, or credentialed we may be.

Chapter one ended with the idea of *reversing the funnel*. That image serves as a metaphor for fluidity as well. When we grow rigidly certain about our knowledge, we are like an upside-down funnel. The wide end (all we *think* we know) excludes new information. What happens? The funnel becomes a helmet. The narrow part tapers to a small opening, like the Tin Man. Imagine trying to pour water (information) through the small opening. As it rains down, it spills. New ideas can't get in to alter our thinking. Most of it washes away. If we celebrate our myopia—ignorance—rather than fear being wrong, we welcome new ideas, new insights, new perspectives. Then, and only then, can we change. The small end of the funnel is our admission of limited understanding; the large end is now open to *everything else*. When the metaphoric funnel is worn not as a helmet but as a conduit for new ideas, we expand possibilities by admitting our limitations.

The most powerful change we can choose, once we start accepting our ignorance, is to **trust lightness** as the theme for learning. The frame of *play* makes our ignorance useful, even necessary. In the Learning Chaos world, games have nothing to do with winning: *we win when we play*. When we compete, that's a different story—we become locked tightly into rules. After all, you can't *win* a game with no rules. Or can you? In the world of games-as-learning, we shift our focus to *play* rather than *win*. That means we can play some games competitively, say soccer and poker, and we do not let that competition bleed over into the classroom. We can become more comfortable with an open-ended result. Nobody has to win to be successful. At that point we can become more fluid in a world that's increasingly ambiguous. If that's the case, haven't we won something worthwhile by not focusing on winning? Without the pressure to win, we can *lighten up*.

Lightness provides the nourishment for fluidity. Rigid frames prevent fluid learning. That's a precept of Learning Chaos. Since humor is always about colliding frames—the breakdown of rigidity—learning lightly prevents frames from shutting down the process. Here's a classic example: *What do you call a veterinarian who only treats one species? A physician.* When we hear the punch line, it's funny because two frames harmlessly collide: doctors and veterinarians as separate categories. This joke also opens up a whole realm of insights about animals, humans, medicine, language, titles, and more. But only if we relax. If we take ourselves too seriously—*holding a dime,* in the vernacular—we don't laugh enough to explore. When we're proceeding lightly, the collision of frames provokes laughter and possibility rather than defensiveness.

Each non-serious breath we take opens up possibility. Humor keeps our thinking light, helps us stay out of frame lockdown, and finds openings—an insight, a movie, a book, or *another person.* Schools tend to be much too serious, seeing regimentation as the cure for chaos. A corrosive impact of that dysfunction is isolation: The classroom from the community. Students from teachers. First graders from second graders. Art and music from academics. Primary school from high school.

Humor removes barriers which are built by the overly serious. How can we expect children, or anyone, to embrace learning when we equate smiling and laughter with a lack of focus? By middle school, we're expected to line up and stop having fun. But fun seeds the field of problem-solving and critical thinking with solutions. Watch the movie, *Ferris Bueller's Day Off.* The principal is monomaniacal in his goal and in his methods, and we see, again and again, where that leads. He can only fail, especially as he tries harder. Ferris, full of chaos and fun, is flexible. He's also successful. Some say the theme of the movie is rebellion. I suggest it's the triumph of fluidity.

Einstein, like Ferris Bueller, is a personal hero. A few years ago I was in Princeton and met a woman working in a corner store. Her mother had worked there when Einstein was a regular customer. She remembered him as a vague and gentle man who had trouble making change. Imagine that! Maybe he was taking shopping lightly. Many of us hold an image of Einstein frantically writing formulas in a cloud of chalk dust. I used to hold that image, too. Then one day a participant in one of my sessions mentioned *combinatory play*. According to Einstein's own journals, combinatory play is how he allowed his theories to find him in his intellectual corner store.

He was practiced at not thinking too hard. Instead, he allowed the answers to arrive when they pleased. He relied on his emotions, memory pictures, his senses, muscular sensations, a whole mélange of nonlinear information, freely accepted and without much direction, to lead him. Once the insight popped up, he started writing. Like Stuart Firestein, Albert Einstein had an appetite for uncertainty, the foggy landscape. The formulas grew from the collision of ideas and feelings. According to Mr. Einstein, the process, "the essential factor in productive thought," looks something like the chart below.

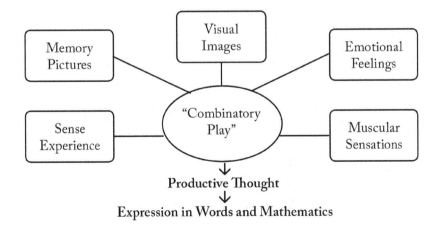

The frame of *play*—rather than the frame of work—may be our greatest asset as humans. It worked for Einstein, and, after all, every game involves critical thinking. Every game engages Daniel Pink's intrinsic motivators: To seek out novelty and challenges, to extend and exercise our capacities, to explore and learn. And as we play and engage in thinking lightly, dropping the dime, shall I say, we realize that **everyone is qualified**.

While teaching a class in job interviewing, I met a very smart man who introduced me to the idea of qualification. He was about to retire and had taken the class out of curiosity. He'd interviewed multitudes over his career as a manager, and he told me, "I never paid much attention to credentials. I mean, beyond a certain number of letters after your name that enabled you to apply, they meant nothing. I focused on qualifications—how did they think like me and not like me?"

No two humans think exactly alike. However many minutes you have been breathing, each moment of your experience is different from mine. Even if we're lifelong friends with the same politics, religion, and favorite sports team. Our differences are often frustrating, sometimes maddening, but if we can appreciate the benefits of divergence, our differences become our greatest source of strength. *Everyone is qualified* means that no one is more of an expert in your experience than you. Not me, not your parents, not your boss, not your therapist.

Though our differences can be ranked—by experience, age, education, for instance—what credentials don't indicate is our unique ability to imagine. Imagination is the active ingredient in fluidity. We can always access each others' imaginations if we let go of preconceptions about credentials and stop assuming data-collecting is of any value at all without imagination to turn it loose. Yet, "in course after course the message is driven home: the quality of your analysis counts for more than the quality of your imagination."[12] Great insight, and great innovations often appear in spite of credentials.[13]

In the 1930s, Chester Carlson, a patent attorney, grew frustrated with the mess and waste of carbon paper. He invented a crude prototype of a device that could create copies. He tried peddling his invention to IBM, 3M, and Kodak. They weren't much interested. He clearly wasn't an expert in the technology. So he started his own company, Xerox.

In 1984, the Breed Corporation tried to sell a device that would serve as a cheap trigger for air bags. The big three auto manufacturers in Detroit were unimpressed by Mr. Breed's credentials: his company specialized in hand grenades. Frustrated, he turned to Japan, where they ignored his credentials and welcomed his imagination.

In the 1980s, Southwest Airlines was experiencing delays in turning their planes around quickly and efficiently, a critical factor in airline success. Rather than trying to copy from other airlines or hiring experts, they went to Nascar and watched pit crews, a group with no airline credentials at all.[14]

My favorite example is Paul MacCready, who twice won the Kremer prize with the Gossamer Condor and the Gossamer Albatross, both human-powered aircraft. The first took off and landed after flying a one-mile oval course. The second crossed the English Channel. In a 1983 Science Digest article, he explained how his lack of expertise worked for him: "My secret weapon was a complete lack of experience in aircraft-wing structural design while, at the same time, having a familiarity with hang gliders and fragile model airplanes. Our competitors also knew about hang gliders, but they were thwarted by knowing so much about standard techniques." He stated in an interview that he got the inspiration for the design when watching his son fly a toy glider. Everyone is qualified.

When we can see through another's eyes, we magnify possibility.

Jonathan Swift defined vision as "the art of seeing what is invisible to others." Allowing new information to challenge our frames of thinking gives us new starting places for seeing, which determines the range of our thinking. Let's look at something highly visible, like the world.

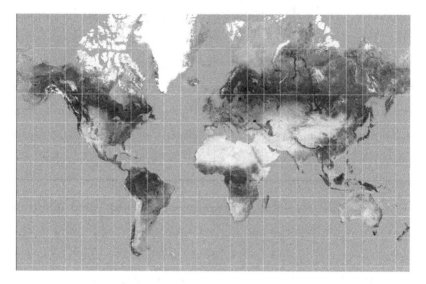

This map adorns most school walls. It's an exceptional map, developed by a fellow named Gerardus Mercator, who discovered an ingenious way to create a cylindrical representation of a globe. Flatten out the cylinder and you have a map. Obviously, that involves some distortion. He made his distortion choices based on what at the time was an urgent need: navigation for sailing ships. His charts make it possible to plot a straight line on a curved surface, the Earth. Very useful when he invented it in 1569. It's an attractive map, and we're used to it, and it may be a bit out of date since it predated the first satellite by almost 400 years. Way before GPS as well.

Many of us, when we think of "world map," think of Mercator's map because we're used to it. On the next page is another map of the world.

This is the Hobo-Dyer map of the world, designed not for sailing but to show the continents in actual relative size. Compare it with Mercator's projection and you'll find some wows. You've just doubled your frames for thinking of "map of the world." Fluidity adds choices; that's what makes it useful. Fluidity also demands more rigor of us since we have to choose. That can feel uncomfortable until we're in the habit.

Here's another map:

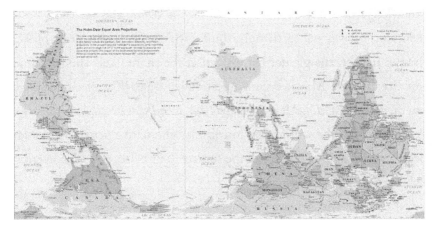

Upside down! Most people exclaim, "But the world is not upside down, is it?" As Buckminster Fuller pointed out, up is not north, up *is*

away from the center of the Earth. You may also notice how our brains are easily fooled, as this map makes it appear that there is more water than land. That's only because of the placement of the Pacific Ocean in the middle of the map. The land-water ratio is the same between the two Hobo-Dyer maps.

It's not information that counts, it's how we frame what we see and hear. *The frame we choose determines the conclusion we reach.* Not the *"facts."* All these maps are equally factual. How, then, can they all be different? *Their difference is what makes them useful because they provide fluid frames.* That's what our schools, our universities, and our corporate trainers need to help us understand: We *see this differently* and t*hat's okay.* What counts is that, as we explore, we keep our thinking *open and fluid.*

So what's the point? It's the most critical point in Learning Chaos. *Discovery, assembly, and skepticism* all support *fluidity.* Instead of answers, we need to focus on questions. Instead of THE WAY, we need to accept different ways. Instead of seeking closure, we need to seek flexibility. Until we do, we're clinging to dinosaurs in prisons. The issue is not knowledge or expertise. The issue is *mental habit.* The smartest, best-educated person on earth only thinks within the boundaries of her frame. In fact, the greater her expertise, the more likely she is to find fluidity difficult. Maybe even to question its value: *Why should I question my own understanding? It defines who I am, why I was hired!* As soon as we lose flexibility, the willingness to consider alternative perspectives as at least interesting—regardless of the source—our biases seize the steering wheel of our comprehension.

Ready for another map?

How about this one, which distorts regions of the world based on a single variable. Compare this one with the map of our old friend, Gerardus Mercator. If you can allow yourself to gasp, you're on the right track. The variable here is population.

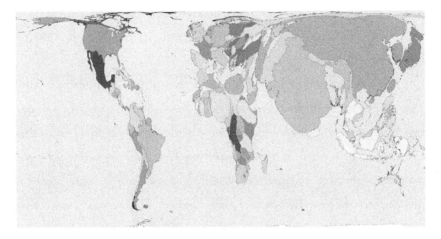

If Gerardus were to come back to us, he might very well figure out the previous map. He was a fluid thinker. However, I doubt he could figure out the one below since it focuses on a variable he couldn't suspect, but that a ten-year-old would easily guess. The variable is *Internet users*.[15]

Like tools in a box, frames give us choices. We tend to use the tools we find most comfortable because of our experience, training, and, most important, the limits of our understanding. Like the world maps, different perspectives enrich our facility, our ability to shift perspectives. When we allow everyone their qualifications and see them as a resource, we give permission for new ideas and we invite confluence—flowing together. Fluidity.

The next section of Learning Chaos lays out how to better involve learners, whether in the classroom or in corporate training. As parents, teachers, professors, and trainers, we can do a better job of preparing those we help. We can start with ourselves: *How have I exercised discovery, assembly, skepticism, and fluidity today? How have I modeled these behaviors for those around me? Who have I encouraged to see things differently from me?* The principles that support Learning Chaos are simple. They also demand courage, lightness, and patience.

—⧟—

1. Eugene Robinson, in his eulogy to William Raspberry: "A Listener, Not a Preacher," *The Washington Post*, July 20, 2012.

2. From Margaret Wheatley, whose book, *Leadership and the New Science*, (Berrett-Koehler, 1999), somehow manages to combine chaos theory, quantum mechanics, and leadership into a very readable and insightful treatise.

3. John Kelly, "Bright-eyed, bushy-tailed and willing to do whatever's necessary to win," *The Washington Post* (John Kelly's Washington, April 10, 2013).

4. G. K. Chesterton (1874–1936), who also said, "The traveler sees what he sees. The tourist sees what he has come to see."

5. Chesterton, *The Social Animal*.

6. From "Wicked Problems in Networking" (*The Inside*r, Dec. 2002).

7. "Tame" and "Wicked" were coined by Horst Rittel and Melvin Webber in "Dilemmas in a General Theory of Planning" in Policy Science in 1973. The article is accessible at *https://www.gatech.edu/resv/cp/6012/42cpr.htm*. They suggested Wicked Problems cannot be avoided, can never have a comprehensive list of possible solutions, and solving them always produces another wicked problem. Tame problems resemble 2 + 2 = 4, and most of our thinking, they assert, is tame, left over from a simpler time, and inadequate today, too rigid and simplistic.

8. Tim Kastelle, in *Book Riffs, Innovation Strategy: Are You Solving a Puzzle or a Mystery?* (May 10, 2012), provides a concise introduction to this difference. He cites Gregory Treverton and Malcolm Gladwell, who are great resources for discussions too long for this book.

9. From *Smithsonian Magazine*, Sept. 2012, by Daniel Simons, Gorillas in the Midst.

10. From *The Diane Rehm Show* on NPR, May 22, 2012.

11. From a 1999 Gallup Poll. For further surprises, check out http://www.11points.com/News-Politics/11_Things_Americans_Wrongly_and_Frighteningly_Believe.

12. Gary Hamel, "Be Your Own Seer," from *Leading the Revolution*, (Plume, 2002).

13. For more about this concept, look into the work of Debra E. Meyerson and Maureen A. Scully, on *Tempered Radicals*. They suggest that innovation always comes from outliers—people who are not part of the central power structure and who use their differences as a springboard for change. Richard Feynman, Lenny Bruce, and Frank Zappa all qualify, though Lenny Bruce was more radical than tempered. Tempered radicals always introduce chaos into systems to great effect.

14. From *Paradigms*, by Joel Barker, (Harper Business, 1992).

15. All maps were downloaded from *www.worldmapper.com* and are used with permission.

5: CREATING A LEARNING CHAOS ENVIRONMENT

You can't make people learn something until they're ready. When they're ready, you can't stop them. The goal of Learning Chaos is to provide a haven for learning. Someplace where it's *safe* to be ready. A space filled with encouragement, challenges, and vulnerability. No wrong answers or correct answers. Just different answers. A classroom that invites an avalanche of questions. To accomplish this, we must first resist the temptation to control others' learning. We must fight the impulse to be right. Knowledge in a Learning Chaos classroom is a byproduct of continuous learning. It is not an end in itself.

I'm not knocking knowledge. *Discovery, assembly, skepticism, and fluidity* drive learning. Knowledge is a key factor in learning. But it's not the sole factor or even the most important factor. Insight—the application of knowledge—is more important. And insight has little chance of blossoming in traditional teaching environments.

When preparing to teach within a traditional framework, our *first thought* will be bound by that framework—the framework of control.

How can I manage what happens in the classroom? From that point on, all our decisions repudiate the themes of Learning Chaos. We're operating within *traditional tenets* that block learning. These outmoded tenets include:

- The instructor is the expert;
- The correct answer is the goal;
- Student learning is the instructor's responsibility;
- Learning is serious business; and
- Classroom order is a priority.

My teacher training was based on these assumptions. I accepted them. Labelled *classroom management*, they were woven into my graduate program. Now, I'm not against management per se. Management works well when applied to finances, technology, errands. *Things.* It's often ineffective when applied to people. Implicit in classroom management is the notion that the teacher's authority rests on controlling the environment—and *the people in it.* Ouch.

"You manage *things*, lead *people*. People are not things. If you treat people like things, you'll piss them off."[1] As a new teacher, I challenged my own assumptions about people and management. From my first day, I chafed under the yoke of *control.* Everything about the school shouted control: the bells, the periods, the setup of the classroom, the teachers' lounge (off-limits to students), three lunch shifts, bus duty. My best learning experiences suggested otherwise. When the traditional tenets stood in my way, I reversed them. Immediately, I began to learn more effectively. That translated into teaching more effectively. I began following the opposite assumptions, which became the tenets for Learning Chaos.

- The experts are in the audience;
- The next question is the goal;
- Everyone's learning is everyone's responsibility;
- Learning is neither serious nor business; and
- Classroom chaos is a priority.

This chapter focuses on developing Learning Chaos habits. How do we do that? By making simple choices every time we are responsible for learning. Although most of my work now is with tall learners (a.k.a. adults), I find the same streams that energize children—discovery, assembly, skepticism, and fluidity—work for adults. The main difference? Adults need more prodding to let go of old habits. Yet no matter the age or experience of a group, they, and we, learn more powerfully when we stand back from our own illusion of authority.

I sometimes find myself reverting to bad habits, especially with authority. It happens most when I see myself as a teacher. Or an expert. Hey, I'm just another learner. When I align myself with the Learning Chaos tenets, I am connected to learning and take myself less seriously. I suggest that whenever you find yourself falling back on a traditional tenet, flip it. Embrace a new frame that better provides for the learning around you. And within you.

—∞∞∞—

"I agree with the sentiments Carl Rogers expressed in *Personal Thoughts on Teaching and Learning.* In essence, he contends that nothing of value can be taught, but that much of value can be learned. I suppose that's one reason I find teaching so unsatisfying and learning so much fun."

—Jerry Harvey

Traditional Tenet #1: The instructor is the expert.
Instructors know the correct answers.

Challenging the instructor is disrespectful.

Students are here to be taught.

If students give the right answer, they've learned.

Learning Chaos Tenet #1: The experts are in the audience.
Instructors question their own answers.

Challenging the instructor shows respect.

Students are here to teach.

When students are confused, they're more likely to learn.

There's nothing wrong with expertise. I especially appreciate the quality in auto mechanics, dentists, and surgeons. Am I suggesting that instructors ignore subject matter? No. However, expertise in *learning* trumps knowledge of subject matter every time. It's far more important for a teacher to know *how to learn* than *how to teach*. Teachers model learning when they are knowledgeable. But not when they see their knowledge as the bottom line. What they have learned is important, it's not *sufficient*. Teachers encourage learning when they show willingness to consider new, different ideas.

I believe we have a responsibility to research like crazy for every topic we present. A wide and deep knowledge about the subject matter, and *about adjacent subjects*, is critical. Why adjacent subjects? Because once we realize that we don't need to control *where* our students go, we prepare for detours and sideways learning. Be patient, be adventurous, and trust that we will come back to the original topic when we're *all* ready. Broad and sustained learning on our part gives us a foundation for dialogue. We can share challenging questions, fearless because *we don't have to know it all.* It gives us the freedom to change the course of the program, on the spot, as the participants' questions and feedback challenge us.

When we challenge the expert, we activate innovation and discovery, great and small. As long as expertise trumps learning, we can expect stagnation. As Learning Chaos learners, we can be comfortable with what we don't know. Expertise is like coolness. If you have to claim it, you don't have it. Relax. Drop the dime. Never mistake your own voice for a higher power.

If you see yourself as an expert, how uncomfortable would you feel if you answered a participant's question with "I don't know"? We teachers fall for the myth that *we must know everything.* "I don't know" makes us accessible and human. Our participants will jump at the chance to help *us* learn. By uttering those three words we become partners in learning. That's a central element of Learning Chaos. What feels like weakness is actually the greatest strength of an instructor who embraces the idea of *letting people learn.* Learning Chaos instructors grow to be daring and transparent about what they know and, more important, what they don't.

We learn the most when a participant challenges something we've tossed their way. We teachers (and trainers, i.e., teachers of tall people) are in the habit of asking a rote question: "Are there any questions?" What we usually mean is, "Is there something anyone forgot to write down?" Since our students—and we—support the myth of the instructor as expert, the important questions never get asked. When no one asks questions, we assume that learning has taken place. Yikes! The absence of questions never indicates that learning has taken place. That absence means that learning has stopped! Learning is an action, not the completion of an action. When we're focused on plowing through content, we don't allow time and room for discovery.

We also sabotage learning by asking questions for which *we already know the answer*:

"So, what do you think this leads to?"

"Who can tell me why this is true?"

"Does anyone know where this term comes from?"

"And what does this mean?"

Closed questions create closed minds. "Question" comes from the same root word as "quest." Question means "to ask," and it also means "to seek." In a Learning Chaos environment we can purposely leave out information. We can even suggest a possibility we think is highly unlikely. How's that for breaking a rule? Students catch on quickly to the game that develops.

A student's first question takes nerve, and it is usually preceded by, "This is probably wrong, but ...." He's apologizing for challenging the teacher. Then he realizes it's okay and an apology is unnecessary. He becomes excited, involved in the dance of discovery that supports his insights, *his expertise*. Then, and only then, is a closed question useful—to check congruence.

It's not easy to back off if you are used to being the person with all the answers. It's not easy to welcome a question if it *feels* like a challenge. Yet only then is it safe for students to learn. Only then is it safe for them to *teach us*. We must have absolute faith in our students; they will get there *if we let them*. Not if we have to *take* them.

In the space between our open questions and their challenges, we can generate the opportunity of ambiguity. Confusion is the motor of learning. We can carry over content and link it with other content—history and physics, conflict and leadership, project management and emotional intelligence. Rather than guide the group toward certainty, it is far more desirable to help them treasure their confusion. Why? Because it leaves space for connections and insight. *Certainty* does not.

———

"Creative thinking may simply mean the realization that there is no particular virtue in doing things the way they have always been done."

—Rudolph Flesch

Traditional Tenet #2: The correct answer is the goal.
The students' job is to regurgitate the *correct answer.*
Every other answer is wrong.
Teachers, trainers, other experts, know the *correct answer.*
Once they tell us the *correct answer*, we can stop looking (and thinking).

Learning Chaos Tenet #2: The next question is the goal.
The students' job is to question—*But what if…?*
Every other answer is a possibility.
Experts only know *their* correct answer.
Whenever we think we've found the correct
answer, we need to be suspicious.

What's the correct way to hold a golf club? To raise a child? To build a house? To fund a business? Lots of people are sure there's a single *correct answer* to these questions. You may have noticed that many of them successfully market instructional videos on the Internet. It's tempting to rely on the *correct answer*, because then we don't have to think anymore.

In the previous chapter I wrote about the urge for certainty as a vestige from our early history, when survival was iffy and threats were real and abundant. The allure of *the correct answer* is dangerous precisely because it implies safety. "I know *the* answer" makes us feel protected. Armored in certainty, we can stop searching, stop questioning, even stop paying attention (learning). Changing the article from "the" to "an"— from "I know *the* answer" to "I know *an* answer"—moves us toward more powerful learning. And isn't the second statement more rational?

Teacher: "Can anyone tell me who Shakespeare was?"
Second grader: "He makes fishing rods!"

The second grader was me, and I was sure of the right answer. I'd been given a Shakespeare™ spinning outfit for my birthday The class laughed, and the teacher reprimanded me for being a wise guy. Was my answer wrong? Yes, according to my teacher. What if her first thought had been "different answer" instead of "wrong answer"?

Oddly enough, the oldest known root of *correct* seems to be two words: *cor* (guide) + *regere* (together). As the word morphed through French, it took on the meaning of *amend, make straight*. What if we teachers and trainers went back to the older meaning and saw *guiding together* as our role? We could steer toward mutual understanding.

By embracing the older meaning, we would understand that others' perceptions are *correct for them at that moment*. That would leave us— parents, teachers, and trainers—free to explore other perceptions. What would happen then? We might gain insight into alternatives. That's what learning is—exploring alternatives. If learning means hitting the *correct answer button* on an expert's teaching machine, we've had it. We become dinosaurs. One-trick ponies. Dead ends.

Let's view learning as looking for *questions*. Answers are merely stepping-stones to the next question. Answers are the beginning, not the end, of learning. The best questions start with "What if?"

Questions take courage. Especially among teaching professionals. In our education and then in our professional life, we buy into a strange dysfunction: "Don't ask questions."

This practice, like most dysfunction, is fertilized by fear. Here's a partial list of why we're afraid:

If I don't know the answer, I'll look stupid.

People are waiting for me to stumble.

Questions challenge core beliefs that I don't want to reconsider.

Questions mean I didn't make my point clear enough.

I'm the teacher; knowing the correct answer is my raison d'être!

Some questions are worth asking:

Why do we put administrators in charge of teachers?

Why should we list objectives at the start of a class?

Why do we break the day up into periods, separated by alarm bells?

Why don't we have the students help make lunch?

I'm willing to bet, if you asked questions like these, you'd hear:

Because that's the way everybody does it.

Because we always have done it this way.

Just get back to work.

Do you have a problem?

Robert Max Jackson, a professor of sociology at N.Y.U., offers a class titled: "What If? The Art and Science of Imagining a Society That Never Was." His class encourages questioning everything and exploring all kinds of possibilities. Maybe every class title should have "What if …" as its premise. When learning = the correct answer, asking new questions isn't just uncomfortable, it's revolting. Answers are *useful* only as benchmarks for new questions. Learning is a continuum, not a destination.

We teachers and trainers can help nurture this garden of questioning by balancing our expertise with entertaining possibilities. We need to shed the feeling that we have to correct others. How about, "My experience suggests …," or "We see this differently." Those statements open doors instead of slamming them in our students' faces. If we wear the straightjacket of correct answers, we separate ourselves from new information and, worse, new ideas. We can't be neutral listeners when our ears are stuffed with the cotton of correctness. If we can't learn *all the time*, how can we expect to teach?

"Creativity," said Henri Matisse, "takes courage." When *correct* bludgeons creativity and possibility, many of us cannot muster the courage to be creative. It may not seem worth the fight. But we can serve ourselves and those around us by allowing unanswered questions to enter the conversation. We can stop heaping rewards on ourselves or others for *getting it right*! We must guide together, accept ambiguity, and question our tendency to think that *correct is better*. I say, be valiantly suspicious of *the correct answer*. Especially when it comes from your own mouth.

Learn to view an answer as no more than a possibility, one of many in a series of insights. It may be worthwhile. Or useful. It is never the finish line. In the classroom, an answer is a place to pause — like a fermata in music — before moving on to the next question. And the next. When we impart that kind of courage to those around us, especially those in our charge (students, children, participants), they will take more care and become more mindful about their own learning. When we accept answers as an end to further exploration, there is no reason to move forward. Why? Because we declared, with self-righteous certainty, "It's over."

The responsibility for learning distributes evenly when no one, and everyone, is in charge.

"School should allow a lot to be learned, which means it should teach little."

—Josef Albers

Traditional Tenet #3: Students' learning is the instructor's responsibility.
The students expect to be taught.
Learning means being talked at or down to.
Sit near an exit.
This too shall pass.

Learning Chaos Tenet #3: Everyone's learning is everyone's responsibility.
The students expect to teach.
Learning means listening equally.
Sit near the action.
This could be fun.

I'm not knocking teachers. I think everyone should teach public school for two years. There would be greater respect for teachers if we all experienced the long hours, low pay, and disregard that come with the job. But why do *we*—teachers, parents, curriculum designers—decide what *they*—students—should learn? Instructors are not the problem. The philosophy that they're responsible for student achievement is faulty. Are doctors responsible for their patients' health? Are automobile manufacturers responsible for how we drive? In the classroom, that philosophy of codependency removes students from the responsibility for their own learning. They're in charge of completing their homework, showing up on time, following the rules. Nothing more.

The dinosaur idea that teachers are responsible for students' learning removes any value in students' self-direction. The message is clear: You can't be responsible for your own learning, *your own future*. We're in charge of you.

I start my Learning Chaos sessions with two lists—"Will" and "Will Not"—about our time together. The last item on the "Will" list: *You will have opportunities to be interested and to have fun.*

I then promise them *I will be interested and have fun.* I don't promise to be *interesting.* I suggest that if they feel bored, they should get over themselves. *You're responsible for your interest, I'm responsible for mine.*

A peeved participant challenged this statement. "That's not right. It's your job to keep us interested!" A great slogan for how ingrained the funnel/regurgitation frame is: *The instructor is responsible for my learning.* During a break, this participant and I had a fruitful conversation. When we returned to the conference room, he introduced some valuable insights to the group, *after* he'd moved past his *learning-as-codependency* frame. Once he'd discarded the first false assumption (*Students expect to be taught),* the other three faded. He engaged, challenged, and, during breaks, spoke about what we were doing rather than escaping to the coffee shop. We were both *equally* excited.

When everyone is involved in *every aspect* of learning, everyone moves forward. Sometimes just metaphorically, but often physically. They move into a place where they can participate. They're checked in. And, as with a good movie, it's over too soon.

Most of us are still chained to the idea that it's cheating to help each other in class. Worse, we buy the idea that the teacher knows more than we do. How nonsensical is that? There are always more students than teachers in the class. Coupled with this curious perspective is the notion that teachers and trainers should learn *before* they enter the classroom. That's not merely bass-ackward, it disqualifies *most of the people in any classroom*. Imagine how many possibilities can blossom if everyone teaches.

Talk with Jabali Sawicki at breakthroughcollaborative.org, a program in which older students, in high school and college, work in learning partnerships with younger students. They maintain a 7:1 ratio. The cost is minimal, and the success is impressive. Or Project-Based Learning, in schools such as Wheaton High School, a suburb of Washington, DC. There, students and faculty work in equal collaboration to explore and solve a real-world task or problem.

Why do people choose to become instructors? I've met few teachers who weren't excited about learning. No one enters teaching to get rich. Or for prestige (except in Finland). I provide learning for a living. I don't have the connections or the marketing machinery to generate business except through referrals. If I can't help people get excited about learning, my phone doesn't ring.

When instructors find ways to bring excitement to learning, accountability is not an issue. It seems that in our effort to promote learning, we're moving in the wrong direction. Instead of evaluating the instructor at the end of a training session, how about asking the participants to *evaluate themselves*? If the participants gave themselves high ratings, that would mean *they learned and that the instructor succeeded*. Currently, no matter how high the ratings an instructor receives, the learners aren't expected to be seekers, they're expected to be recipients—voids waiting to be filled. How about ditching on-the-spot evaluations altogether? How about ditching grades? (There's a concept worth exploring!) Are there any data that indicate grades support learning?

> *"At the University of Southern California, a leadership course was taught each year to fifty of the most outstanding students of twenty-seven thousand in the school, hand-picked by each department. At the end of the semester, the grader for the course was instructed to give one-third of the students A's, one-third B's, and one-third C's—even though the work of any member of this class was likely to surpass that of any other student in the university. Imagine the blow to the morale of the eager and hard-working student who received the requisite C."[2]*

We have an obligation to establish learning as the primary focus in every organization rather than to impose grades and evaluations. Grades imply that we know what people should learn. Evaluations suggest that gathering data—always subjective, including the statements and questions—has some attachment to what people learned that made a difference *to them*. The people who set up evaluations, no matter how well educated and intentioned, are measuring what's important *to them*. In a Learning Chaos classroom, evaluation is internal and self-directed:

I'm excited about what happened today and looking forward to tomorrow. In a Learning Chaos space, where everyone teaches and everyone learns, that environment is fearless and fun.

"Could we use a full understanding of play as a critique, helping us to liberate our best capacities from unnecessary control and regimentation?"

—Pat Kane, *The Play Ethic*

Traditional Tenet #4: Learning is serious business.

Fun disrupts successful learning.

Organize schools like factories.

We need more rules.

The best students follow the rules.

Learning Chaos Tenet #4: Learning is neither serious nor business.

Fun generates successful learning.

Let schools morph.

Any rule that prevents fun should be toilet-papered.

The best students break the rules.

Teaching is business. Education is business. Schools are businesses. Writing books about learning is a business. And learning? Oh, that's *very serious business.* Malarkey!

I have had instructors who used humor in the classroom. Usually, it was pretty ham-handed. Limited to jokes. Some of the instructors were good enough to do stand-up. But I've had few instructors who had, and encouraged us to have, FUN (the other "F" word).

Before I left my last position in a public school system, I took on a summer assignment that included working with two teachers from another department. We were instructed to blend health education curriculum with our specific *disciplines*—that choice of words tells you about fun in academia, right? My two wonderful partners and I worked well together. We had a ball, taking frequent breaks, working on our feet while roaming the campus, launching ideas like kites, and sitting down only to discuss what we'd learned. After a few days, my supervisor corralled me in the hall. (At least she had the decency not to ask me for my hall pass.)

"I've been checking on the other groups," she said. "They are sitting at their desks working hard. Every time I see you three, you're outside or having fun. Don't let me see that again!" So we made sure she never did.

When do we learn the most? When do we delight in discovery? When do we have the most fun? When we're children. If the business of education focused on learning instead of profit, it would measure *fun* as the chief variable of improvement. Because *when we have fun, we learn faster, deeper, and longer.*

Truancy is a problem. Violence in schools is a problem. Bullying is a problem. But fun is not the opposite of good attendance or safety—nor has it ever been. Being serious does not help us solve serious problems. Being serious (from *serius*: *heavy* or *weighty*) limits our flexibility, curiosity, and our capacity to learn. When we're serious, we don't smile.[3] When we don't (or can't) smile, we can't expand. The less fun we're having, the less ability we have to see possibility.

It carries over into the workplace. Many adults, when candid, admit there's an unwritten rule: *We get paid to work because we're supposed to be miserable.* Suppose your supervisor walks in and finds you and some coworkers in hysterics. What do you think happens next?

Regularly, I ask my participants to try an experiment. *Let's all laugh, really laugh, for ten seconds.* I start by laughing as raucously as I can. Perhaps 20 percent of the room is willing to try it. Some cross their arms and frown at this imposition on their cozy world of dourness. These are, after all, *serious* professionals. When I tell them that little children laugh up to 400 times a day and most adults fewer than 30, they appear wistful. And somewhere between the first break and lunch, they begin to trust me and their peers enough to let down their guard. From that point, the light bulbs start firing and laughter ignites learning.

Once, I was working with a group grappling with serious issues in their workplace—turf problems, and a lack of trust between management and administrative support. I listened while they vented for an hour, then asked if they would trust me to lead them in a couple of activities. Half an hour later, we were having fun. So much fun that we drew a couple of stiffs working in a nearby classroom. When they shushed us, I tiptoed to their class. My suspicion was confirmed. Yep, they were doing some "serious training." They sat in rows, stone-faced and rigid as robots, while another robot talked *at* them. The room had the energy level of a snail convention.

Meanwhile, my group produced some creative, and very effective, plans to take back to the office. A few months later, they reported real progress. I take credit only for creating a place where it was safe and useful to have fun. They did the rest. Never once did they ask me what they should do. *Having fun together produces trust, excitement, and camaraderie so that the participants can take responsibility for their own learning.*

What if we defined the *best students* not as those with the highest GPA—though that is a challenging and worthy achievement—but as those who learned with the most excitement and challenged the rules? The ones who found ways to have fun? How about having a *laughometer* in every classroom that broadcasts into the principal's office. When the meter falls below a certain decibel level, the principal steps out of the office to investigate *what is wrong*. When learning is fun, we embrace a lifetime of learning.

I hope you never, ever chide someone for laughing in class.

—⊗⊗⊗—

"Things are always best seen when they are a trifle mixed-up, a trifle disordered. The chilly administrative neatness of museums and filing cases, of statistics and cemeteries, is an inhuman and anti-natural kind of order. It is, in a word, disorder." —Camilo José Cela

Traditional Tenet #5: Classroom control is a priority.
Arrange the room in a grid.
Planning is the key to effective learning.
Give everyone the same instruction.
Stay on topic.

Learning Chaos Tenet #5: Classroom chaos is a priority.
Let the learners arrange the room.
Preparation is the key to effective learning.
Meet everyone in her/his own country.
Let them steer.

Neatness has its advantages. Especially *after learning has taken place*. Too many messages about school—and work—focus on control. Some of them are subtle. Lines in parking lots. Sidewalks. Straight corridors. Chairs in rows. Teacher at the front (facing the *opposite* direction from the students). That kind of constriction gets multiplied by lesson plans, objectives, and bells: *Class is over; stop learning right now!*

Class is never over. Except when learning is narrow and regimented. That may work with ants and bees. Tight control makes sense in a hive. But if our goal is to change minds toward possibilities, we first need to change our own minds about boundaries. Of all the traditional tenets, this one—control—is the most insidious. If we were still preparing children to work in factories, there might be some sense to that approach. Preparing children to assemble cars may not be adequate in the world of the Internet. Tight control in the classroom is like the human appendix—we still have it even though we don't need it.

When we learn to release our own creativity by preparing diligently and learning continually, we announce that it's all right to wander, be messy—and clean up afterward. In other words: to think more, and to plan less.

Let's plan loosely and release the future to our students. Imagine for a moment if a teacher, instead of saying, "Today we will cover Mark Antony's funeral oration," had said, "I'd like to get to Mark Antony's funeral oration today. Maybe." That kind of imprecise goal (and wording) allows us to *prepare*. Then we can proceed and go farther afield within a relaxed framework. When we focus too tightly on control, we don't give our brains room to *storm*—to move past boundaries into relationships among ideas.

Note the natural progression that connects the following: *Politics. Overconfidence. Obituaries. Saying one thing and doing another. Using grief to ignite others' passions. Grief and anger. People at funerals are emotionally vulnerable—a breeding ground for inciting a mob. What does this say about*

Mark Antony's cleverness and the naiveté of Brutus and Cassius? Who had more emotional intelligence, Brutus or Mark Antony? Anywhere we wander with the speech gives us opportunity for insight. In other words: *I'll assist with the ride, and I don't need to steer.*

That's preparation, pure and simple. We can only begin to prepare when we don't over-plan. This may deeply offend and frustrate those who live by Plan = Success. My recipe is a drop of planning, a gallon of preparation. When we plan too much, we actually prepare less. Why? Because we fall into the false sense of security that control breeds. If we've already scripted the direction the class will take, why bother preparing? We plan so that *any thing* won't happen; we prepare so that anything can.

Every student, *like every teacher*, is different. Students need honest opportunity to learn at their own pace, through their own best vehicle for understanding. If we control the direction of learning for our students, they don't learn to *arrange* learning for themselves. The most useful gift we can give them is a clear understanding about how each one learns best—as individual learners, not as part of an assembly line. At any given moment, some need to see it to get it; some to hear it; and others, to do it. Some prefer learning alone, some work best in groups, some in pairs. Some blossom when they mentor. Some work best when they feel a strong sense of independence; others require lots of guidance. Mix and match. Save instruction and dispense it as needed. We need to give learners gentle clues and cues for unearthing their own questions.

> *"And in those moments when we show up, I think those are the most powerful meaning-making moments of our lives even if they don't go well. I think they define who we are."*
>
> —Brené Brown

The Learning Chaos Setup

Children love to learn, and show it. No wonder envy tints our joy and we feel nostalgic when we watch kids playing. They're having so much fun learning! And, although this book focuses primarily on rigidity in schools, adult classrooms—training centers, retreats, colleges—suffer from the same stultifying effect of too much *control*. Who among us has not been rendered somnolent from "death by slides"?

While I have worked with children for most of my professional life, in the past twenty years I've found a home, so to speak, with adults. My company, AzaLearning, serves 180 clients around the country. Among them are warehouse workers, senior executives, rising managers, new hires, and everyone in between. Practicing what I preach, I employ discovery, assembly, skepticism, and fluidity as the core of all my leadership training. I'm here to tell you, Learning Chaos can thrive in training centers as well as it does in elementary schools.

Though taller, adults are capable of the same enthusiasm and sense of adventure as children. First they must be given the opportunity. As in a play, you have to set the scene. Providing a hospitable setting is an imperative first step for learning. Have you ever tuned out in the first five minutes of a class because it was set up to impose boundaries? Or perhaps the leader whispered or spoke in a monotone. Or remained seated throughout the session, made no eye contact, talked at you, or, worst of all, down to you? We've all been there, and it's not something most of us wish to repeat.

First impressions count. Within the first couple of minutes, participants get one of two messages. Either, "Same stuff, different day," or "Something different is happening." Participants may come in with an expression that says "I dare you to get my attention or say anything remotely worthwhile." They are smart and observant, and they catch on fast. Even die-hard cynics can shed their attitude when the instructor sheds his or hers.

It's your job to create a welcoming Learning Chaos environment. During my career I have learned several worthwhile practices for doing this. When working with adults, I strongly recommend removing five key impediments to learning.[4]

Lecterns

Burn them. I'm not insensitive to the plight of unemployed lectern builders. In fact, they could find work as Learning Chaos facilitators.

Lecterns limit our vulnerability. A lectern is a shield. Parking behind one implies that the instructor needs protection. From what? The subtle yet powerful message: "It's me versus them." Lose the lectern. Don't plant yourself in front of the room. Be brave! Move around. Become part of the learning community. How we dress, where we stand, and whether we sit or not, severs or serves our connection to our fellow learners.

Lecterns also obscure our humanity. A lectern implies a hierarchy—instructors are superior to students. Always bear in mind that you, and everyone else in the room, are partners. The experts are in the audience. So, until the instructor joins the group, s/he's not involved in learning.

Lecterns diminish our courage. Lecterns are barriers protecting you from modeling the bravery you need to enter the challenging, exciting chaos of learning. You might as well carry a whip and a chair than to hide behind a lectern. Like any shield, a lectern suggests you need protection from the class. Or maybe from learning.

Microphones

Microphones have their place. They're useful for concerts, crowd control, auditoriums, and annoying your neighbors. They have no place in a learning environment. With a bit of training, you can develop your voice to fill a large training facility—and even reach the cheap seats where the "bad kids" sit.

The human voice is a marvelous instrument. Microphones restrain our power. Electronically compressing that voice delivers a message that is lifeless and distorted.[5] Invest in voice training. Using a microphone does to your voice what wearing a mask does to your facial expressions. Sounding loud and distorted evokes weakness, not power.

Microphones also weaken our connection to our co-learners. You become an announcer, an MC, a distant figure of authority. Using a mic removes you from the chaotic environment of learning, which is ideally about relinquishing, not increasing, control. Perhaps if *everyone* in the room had a microphone, you'd all be equal. And being more *like everyone else in the room* is learning leverage; the microphone imposes distance and separation.

Using a microphone discourages exploration. It provides an electronic hiding place. True learning is risky. It occurs between, not within, havens. You're not a tour guide, you're a fellow explorer. The physical act of using your own unadorned, unenhanced voice encourages everyone else in the room to work without a net.

Seating in Rows

Too many training officers assume this is the only "right way" to set up the classroom. The only benefit I see: it makes taking roll easier. It also shouts, "Stay inside your area at all costs!" Occasionally, I have to get special permission to move tables and chairs from tight little rows to open seating. Honest! As if doing so might threaten national security. That resistance always astonishes me. Maybe the point is to prevent learning, but I prefer to think it's a classic case of "Old habits die hard."

Seating in rows curbs collaboration. Worth repeating is that we're so programmed to avoid collaboration in class that helping each other is considered cheating. We expand our learning universe through connection with diverse points of view. Rows are barriers to collaboration: *You stay in your row, I'll stay in mine.* Such physical constraint provides a constant reminder to not think, merely obey.

Rows constrain freedom. The physical message is: "There is only one correct way/lesson to learn. Let's not risk straining our mental necks by seeking ideas." Sitting in random groups gives everyone permission to learn without restrictions. How we sit in a room provides a jumping-off point for a conversation about perspective: *Why do we still do it that way?*

Rows shackle thinking. Rows are lines that scream "straight-line" thinking. They discourage exploring options, and limit interaction. Learning is a collaborative, relational activity. Others' points of view enrich ours. Rows make us passengers—passive, along for the ride—or, worse, hens in a coop.

The Syllabus

A rough outline is sufficient. You don't need a detailed syllabus or pages of annotated notes (or, God forbid, a rehearsed speech with all the pauses and inflections highlighted in yellow). The learners need to have their hands on the wheel if they're to steer. If they're not steering, they're not learning.[6]

A syllabus restricts flexibility. If the instructor is in control, the students are codependents. They are followers, not leaders in the process of learning, so why should they bother to learn? Ask them what *their* syllabus is. *What are you looking for today?* If they feel a need for more structure, suggest some ideas and, with their help, flesh it out. Not preparing a syllabus does not equal a lack of preparation. It takes *more* consideration and care to prepare for possibilities and ambiguity than to write and print out a syllabus. The energy we put into preparing a syllabus reduces the energy we have for preparing to learn.

A syllabus removes the need for courage. If instructors can't work outside the boundaries of a syllabus, they won't recognize when learning opportunities—chaos—appear. Like a human skeleton, the syllabus provides a framework for *living* tissue—the learning process.

A syllabus restricts collaboration. Teachers—from kindergarten to postgraduate school—aren't smarter or less smart than their students. Every bit of experience an instructor brings to class is matched by an equally valuable, though different, experience brought by each learner. Billie Holiday said, "I never sing a song the same way twice." The same applies to any class. Each class is generated by the particular and temporary group.

Objectives

I never use course objectives with my participants. This drives training officers crazy. When one asks, "What's the purpose of this activity?" I answer, "It depends on what they get out of it." In a Learning Chaos session, *the participants* develop the objectives. Who's responsible for meeting these objectives? *They are.*

Objectives block accountability. They imply that the instructor is responsible for getting the participants to a uniform destination. In fact, every person in the room will take away a slightly, sometimes hugely, different learning. That happens regardless of the instructor's heavy hand, so why not embrace what is, instead of what we think should be?

Objectives trample on the moment. The Learning Chaos environment focuses on the present—a fluid, continuously developing moment of learning that is energetic, opportunistic, and never the same twice. Watch little children, the world's best Learning Chaos proponents. They'll do the same thing over and over and over again. Why? Because for them, it's never the same way twice.

Objectives limit instructors' learning. Without a list of objectives, instructors are free to learn rather than teach. Their spontaneous insights inflame the learning passions of everyone. When participants realize the instructor is eager to learn *from them*, they become energized, involved, relaxed, and courageous.

The first few moments in a classroom set the boundaries and rules before you open your mouth. Let those moments exclaim: *Anything might happen here!*

Learning is the central paradox in being human. We learn whether we want to or not. Learning provides direction, and it can't be directed. Though many things can be taught, the important things can only be learned. When we are assigned to teach, to instruct, we are given a special gift. Accept the gift with grace, enthusiasm, and the courage to follow where learners need to go.

Have patience with everything unresolved in your heart

and try to love the questions themselves ...

Don't search for the answers,

which could not be given to you now,

because you would not be able to live them.

And the point is, to live everything.

Live the questions now.

Perhaps then, someday far in the future,

you will gradually, without even noticing it,

live your way into the answer.

—Rainer Maria Rilke

1. Quoted from a conversation with a wonderful learner named Bill Taggart. He spoke to a group in a leadership program I was facilitating. When I shared the quote with him and asked permission to use it, he asked, "Did I say that?"

2. Rosamund Stone Zander and Benjamin Zander, *The Art of Possibility.*

3. Ron Gutman, "The Hidden Power of Smiling," on TED, is an engaging, brief explanation of lightness.

4. I am working on short papers and blogs on using Learning Chaos principles for different topics, how to generate slides that capture Learning Chaos principles, and more. The LC series will be coming soon, as well as blogs at learningchaosblog.com.

5. If you have trained extensively with microphones, have a top-quality mic and PA system, you can achieve some pretty lifelike quality. But it's rare. In your experience, how many times has a microphone and PA system detracted from a presentation? I thought so.

6. I use outlines of my courses for marketing purposes. People who hire me need something to visualize so they can make a decision regarding my services. I keep these general and process-focused, i.e., the kinds of interactions and learning experiences that are my goal rather than a minute breakdown of content.

CPSIA information can be obtained
at www.ICGtesting.com
Printed in the USA
BVHW041324010520
579049BV00017B/1589

9 780996 301800